# Survival of Life

OntosScience Press—St. Louis, Missouri, USA
ISBN: 979-8-218-24096-7
Title: *Survival of Life*
Library of Congress Control Number: 2023914155
Author: Robert Wheeler, PhD
Digital distribution | 2023
Paperback | 2023
Printed in the United States

www.ontosscience.com

# Survival of Life

Robert Wheeler, PhD

# Contents


Preface ........................................................ ix

Introduction .................................................. xi

1. Can Life Survive? .......................................... 1

2. Second Enlightenment ...................................... 9

3. Ontological Imperative .................................... 17

4. Spirituality .............................................. 23

5. Transcendence ............................................. 39

6. Reality .................................................... 45

7. Basic Constituent ......................................... 51

8. Pragmatic Pluralism ....................................... 59

9. Motivation ................................................ 65

10. Purpose of Life .......................................... 73

11. Purpose in Life .......................................... 83

12. Meaning in Life.......................................... 91

Epilogue ...................................................... 99

Glossary ...................................................... 103

References .................................................... 107

Author ........................................................ 117

Index ......................................................... 123

# Preface

We all have built into us a need to continue daily life with comfort and manageability. This is supplemented with varying degrees of awareness of a deeper need for explanation and improvement of existence. For many people, these latter needs are overshadowed by the former needs of daily life. People are dominated with the daily needs of immediate existence, but usually at some time during their life questions arise about explanation. A colorful sunset or an inspiring concert may trigger wonder of meaning, purpose, and source. For many these deeper questions emerge at about the time of puberty. This is normally a time when the brain has developed the ability for abstract thinking, and experiences have developed sufficiently to cause recognition of conflicts in available information and learning.

For me, the desire for and pursuit of knowledge about these deeper concerns of meaning, purpose, and source started in early teenage years and continued off and on throughout a ninety plus life span. This book is about what I have learned and why it is important, and it is my fourth attempt to publicize the results of my experiences. It is my largesse, my contribution to society, to the advancement of civilization, and to the development of our species, idealistic goals that I am convinced are embedded in all of us somewhere. Despite the idealistic abstract nature of this goal, I am convinced it is an underlying destiny in us all. Hopefully, this book will inspire you to also think about these deep concerns and likewise try to make a long-range contribution to humanity.

This book is mainly about survival of life in general, but that involves views about personal survival. There are many theories, beliefs, and views about what happens to a person's vitality after death, but none are scientifically supported. We really just do not know. The view supported here is that the most important aspect of personal survival is what that person leaves here on earth after physical death, what was contributed, the largesse. These are the footprints left in the sands of time.

> "Footprints that perhaps another,
> Sailing o'er life's solemn main,
> A forlorn and shipwrecked brother,
> Seeing shall take heart again."
> (A Psalm of Life, Wadsworth)

# Introduction

The view that a person has of a goal that supplies meaning and purpose in life was popularized by the famous Austrian psychiatrist Viktor Frankl (1997) as a result of his experiences in a Nazi prison during the holocaust of World War II and in his psychiatric practice. As a prisoner he observed that holocaust prisoners that had a goal beyond mere survival endured the rigors of incarceration better than those without any such goal, and during his psychiatric practice he observed that a large portion of his patients suffered from a lack of having a sense of purpose in their lives. Much research has supported his theory and it has been incorporated into modern psychology and psychiatry (Hooker, Masters, & Park; 2017).

This book expands the role of an individual's view of purpose in personal life to the more important role of an individual's view of the purpose of life in general and the relationship of that view to the individual's own purpose in personal life and the impacts. It starts in Chapter 1 with a brute explanation about the predicted terminal destiny of life supported by science, philosophy, and religion with the question of the fate of human life as we know it. Science tells us that within one billion years the sun will have expanded causing the ultimate climate change that will destroy life on earth (Shah, 2021; Helmenstine, 2021). Most religions and cultural ideologies also predict a cessation or transformation of human life on earth. A survey of history shows a pattern of continual increase in complexity and sophistication of nature that led to human life and raises the question of whether this pattern of development will continue and if it will produce a form of life that can survive the cessation of our current physical existence. This is elaborated on with the subsequent chapters.

Chapter 2 shows that major changes are now taking place similar to major changes that took place during earlier stages of history. The Axial age and the Enlightenment period were important stages laying the groundwork for religions and ideologies that advanced civilization and still dominate societies. Chapter 3 points out that these changes result from a concern about existence and its explanation that is innate to human nature; however, conscious consideration of this concern has become over-shadowed by concern with immediate daily needs such as wealth, comfort, influence, and entertainment. The submergence of these innate deep concerns has decreased the benefits of traditional religions and stimulated the spirituality movement explained in Chapter 4 as an attempt to restore these benefits. Chapter 5 points out that pursuing this long-range idealistic goal may seem pointless, but it is an innate drive, and currently some organized attempts toward that goal are underway.

Chapter 6 then explores various views of reality resulting from these attempts to explain deep concerns. This is further discussed in Chapter 7 with information from sub-atomic physics about the basic constituents of our physical world that help to explain reality and the importance of that explanation.

Personal outlooks, attitudes, worldviews, and philosophies that facilitate the pursuit of these deep concerns are presented in Chapter 8. Chapter 9 discusses the role of thinking about these deep concerns and how that thinking motivates actions and supplies energy to meet more immediate needs.

Chapter 10 proposes that information in the preceding chapters supports the theory that the purpose of life (POL) is to develop personally, collectively, and species wide contributing to nature's increasing complexification and sophistication. Chapter 11 points out that it follows from the POL that a person's individual sense of purpose in personal life (PIL) is to pursue that POL with goals relevant to each individual person. Chapter 12 brings it all together showing that pursuing a PIL based on a POL supplies a sense of meaning in life (MIL) which has been found to be an important factor for health, well-being, performance, and satisfaction for individuals and peaceful relations for nations.

Many references to sophisticated information with citations are presented to support major points in each chapter. These are only samples of reliable information available. They are used to show that the points are more than merely the author's ideas, that they have scientific support. If you are not concerned with scientific support, the cited information can be skipped. Please do not become inundated with supporting information and lose the major points.

An epilogue is added because the author could not resist making comments about his elderly status and the importance of considering these long-range idealistic questions in order to insure a sense of satisfaction with life. Hopefully, this will ensure that you can avoid a feeling of despair and pointlessness. And finally, a glossary is added to clarify the use of terms that may be confusing, and to formally define some new terms.

This is a sobering view of human life involving long-range idealistic goals. Most people have difficulty focusing on current short-term goals like getting a regular paycheck, and discount these long-rang goals as being impractical. Why be concerned about what will happen a billion years from now when what will happen a year from now is difficult to manage? The answer supported in this book is that if we all thought more about these long-rang goals and less about our personal wealth, comfort, influence, and entertainment, most of the current world problems would be alleviated. How different attitudes and outlooks would be if our media, leaders, politicians, and educators emphasized these long-range idealistic goals over the current emphasis on violence, conflict, power, wealth, and entertainment. Results would be the replacing of competition for self-centered goals with cooperation and benevolence. The increasing incidence of depression, anxiety, suicide, and dissatisfaction in individuals would be reversed; crime, murder, robbery, and violence in societies would diminish; and global terrorism, aggression, and warfare would cease. Pursuing such long-range goals and deep concerns in the past has propelled the development of human life and civilization. Renewing this pursuit will inspire a renewed direction and energy for daily activities and restore a sense of satisfaction with personal life.

For our ancient ancestors, life was mysterious and fragile. They thought a lot about reasons for their existence and about activities to improve survival that involved deep concerns about whys and wherefores. Because objective scientific information was so limited, they developed explanations based on assumptions forming religions and ideologies that still dominate cultures. These traditional religions, ideologies, and cultures provided many benefits that have decreased recently because of conflicts with modern experiences and research findings. To update these explanations and restore benefits of religion, we need to think about deep concerns once again. Yes, this is a long-range on-going idealistic effort, but while that effort is being pursued just redirecting some of the energy currently devoted to wealth, influence, comfort, and entertainment to these deep concerns would alleviate world problems. Furthermore, if we do not think about these deep concerns, human activities may shorten the available time, and life could cease prematurely because of things like nuclear explosion, over-population, and pollution.

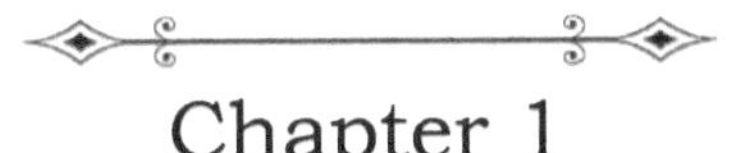

# Chapter 1
## Can Life Survive?

We all agree that the basic goal of life is survival. This means sustenance and reproduction, food and sex. Even though societies have been concerned throughout known history with belief in high level things like salvation or transcendence, survival has been a dominant concern. Physical existence will become even more of concern because science now predicts that within about four billion years physical existence on Earth will be burned to a crisp, and human life will probably have ceased within about one billion years because of the ultimate global warming over which we have little control. This is when the sun will have expanded and created the ultimate climate change (Shah, 2021; Helmenstine, 2021). Most religions also predict a cessation of current human life or change that produces some form of altered existence. In theology this is known as eschatology, study about the end of life on earth.

What will happen at that time to human life? Does that mean that life as we know it will not survive? New information coming from physics, cosmology, psychology, and philosophy is producing new ideas about life, particularly human life, that clouds previous predictions. Is science finding that life may be more than physical existence that will burn to a crisp? Could a form of life emerge that survives this destruction of physical matter or maybe that becomes a new creation as proposed in many religions, especially Christianity (Hausoul, 2019)?

Quantum physics that explains nicely observations of sub-atomic particles has opened science to considerations previously reserved for philosophy and religion. The physical environment in which we live has been found to consist of forces and particles that in turn consist of energy forms and fields of nebulous nature. It seems that to explain some recent observations something even more basic than this is involved, something such as intelligence, information, or consciousness (Wheeler, 1997). This implies that our physical world at its most basic level may be non-physical and consequently not subject to physical destruction. (More on this is in Chapter 6.) When the sun destroys all physical material on earth, could something remain that possibly would build new particles in a different environment, maybe a new creation? Could human life evolve to a different form that would survive in a different reality? Most religions provide for this, but until recently science has provided no support.

Recent studies of complexity supply a possible scientifically supportable avenue for this scenario. A pattern that jumps out from history and paleontology is the repeated emergence of more complex levels of components in the universe. This could be the result of creative design, or it could result from natural evolution with implications discussed in Chapter 10. In any case, shortly after the Big Bang mysterious forces melded to form atoms with increased complexity and new emergent characteristics that were more than the "sum of its parts" (McCall, 2010).

Next on the scale of complexity are molecules which are combinations of atoms that once again melded in a mysterious way and likewise interacted to form more complex chemical compounds. As molecules interacted with each other another mysterious thing developed, life. Molecules in combination learned to reproduce and melded into complex organizations that facilitated existence and reproduction. This is studied by the field of biology that now admits that the mysterious way that life starts and proceeds is influenced by unknown factors, and that the emergence of life cannot be explained by looking only at its basic parts (Service, 2015).

Living systems of molecules combined to form vegetation, animals, and ultimately humans with ever increasing complexity. The field of biology gave way to the various fields of human physiology and psychology that are making strides in explaining the fascinating ways in which the human body grows, reproduces, and declines. A special feature of human life is the brain which is more complex than any other known thing. The new field of neuroscience combines many classic fields to study how the brain operates, how it produces the mind with sophisticated capabilities of information processing that vastly improved survivability; and how the mind produces consciousness, an awareness of mind processes that produces concerns about the process itself, why it exists, what its purpose is, and its future (Jeeves & Brown, 2009). Personal consciousness has been found to interact with both internal body processes and external factors such as other people, things, and external sources of information (Radin, 2006). Fascinating new findings are continually being announced, but as more is known deeper mysteries involving unknown factors and possibilities develop.

The next level of complexity developed as humans realized their dependence on each other. Like molecules, they self-organized into groups that facilitated existence and reproduction. Collections of socialized individuals produced sophisticated cultures that continued the pattern of increasing complexity of nature. The fields of anthropology, sociology, and history have demonstrated a continuing human development that advanced civilization and culture in both efficiency and complexity (Baumeister, 2005).

Anthropology is the field of study that has supplied most information about human development. Different researchers have proposed different timelines and stages; however, most agree that our unique line of descent started about seven million years ago when a group of higher primates emerged with a larger brain capacity that enabled them to find food more efficiently (Pfeiffer,1969). Brain capacity and cognitive ability continued to develop, and three million years ago "homo erectus" emerged with the ability to travel away from its habitat. Its members moved beyond their native environment in Africa meeting new challenges that further increased brain capacity and cognitive ability. By 100,000 years ago they had multiplied forming societies considered the first civilizations in Egypt, Mesopotamia (Iraq), and India. Shortly thereafter they expanded to China and Australia, and about 15,000 years ago reach the Americas. This required a lot of courage and cognitive ability because they did not have autos, ships, or airplanes. Archeologists that do the foot work for anthropologists indicate that religious activity had started by then to support the Christian dogma about humans being created about 10,000 years ago. That was when the sophisticated human thinking ability emerged. As cognitive ability and knowledge increased, language developed and by 5,000 years ago writing and city-states had begun. Another milestone was about 3,000 years ago when religious organizations emerged followed by the start of Christianity 2,000 years ago.

It is well established that the complexity and sophistication of human thinking has developed over time. The earliest known forms of thinking attributed animal and human characteristics to supernatural forces that could account for existence. This resulted in the superstitious beliefs of animism and shamanism that became more sophisticated with time and developed into religions and ideologies. In addition to explaining the cause of mysterious phenomena, these systems met many other needs such as ordering community activities, establishing acceptable behavior, and providing physical and mental support. Most importantly they provided a culture of conduct, ethics, and morals that were exemplified in behavior, the things people did.

Around the period from 700BCE to 200BCE major changes had occurred in cognitive ability and belief systems that laid the foundations for the major religions of today. Laozi started Taoism emphasizing a harmonious naturalness; Confucius laid the foundation for social humanism; Buddha gave people power to influence their future; Zoroaster introduced original goodness that must be reclaimed; Judaism was revitalized with miraculous events; and Greek philosophy was organized. This period has been termed the "Axial Age" and seemed to result from the development of sophisticated abilities to consider new situations and events without primitive superstitions (Armstrong, 2000). Christianity and Islam grew out of these movements.

By the eighteenth-century CE, these religions had become so well established that cultures with dogma, faith, worship had difficulty adjusting to growing knowledge setting the stage for another major change in belief systems and culture, the Enlightenment. This was an age of revolt against authoritarian political and religious powers that conflicted with the advance of knowledge, new experiences, and objective thinking. The world had emerged from the "dark ages" and was adjusting to new-found freedom, knowledge, and prosperity. The major religions that survived adjusted also (Armstrong, 2000).

Studies of history and paleontology show a continual development in nature toward increasing complexity that enables more effective ways of existing. We modern day humans are the result of this process. There is a pattern of emergent capabilities that seems to have purpose and design. Whether this was the result of a supernatural Great Creator, or the result of a mysterious evolutionary process, is not as important as realizing that this advance of nature occurred. Primordial forces combined to form atoms which combined to form molecules which, in turn, combined to form living cells which combined to form animals from which developed humans. Humans with their mental abilities combined to form societies and civilization. A purposeful pattern of increasing complexity is indicated. So, here we are, people with sophisticated mental abilities that realize we are part of a developing pattern that seems to be pointed to increasing complexity—a continuing process.

It took millions of years for living organisms to emerge with a brain capable of processing information, and then many more years to emerge with the use of conscious awareness that we have today. Science indicates that about one billion years are available for further development of human life and if past increases in complexity continue, other forms of life may emerge in that time. It is even possible that as solar heat builds up, human adaptability may overcome characteristics subject to material destruction of nature and continue in a post-solar system. If the basic constituent of matter is non-material (consciousness, information, intelligence, super-mind, etc. explained in Chapter 6) as indicated by recent findings in sub-atomic physics, could a form of life emerge that is not affected by the destruction of matter? It is a long shot, but already human efforts are showing potential explained in Chapter 5.

It is well established that the complexity of human thinking has developed over time. When religions developed, life acquired purpose and explanation. Even the non-believers were subjected to the prevailing culture that established acceptable behavior and direction for actions in their society. Unfortunately, as previously explained, modern experiences and research findings are shaking the foundations of traditional religions to such an extent that their benefits are being lost.

Major changes are occurring in religions to make their beliefs more sensible and reclaim their benefits, but if we are going to continue for a billion more years and surmount physical constraints, we must do more by renewing the type of thinking pursued by our distant ancestors that developed first explanations of existence. Those explanations need updating. Just the process of pursuing updating efforts and adopting such thinking would alleviate most of today's problems in the world. It would stimulate a constructive sense of purpose that would reduce discontent, depression, and anxiety for individuals. For societies it would reduce violence, crime, and murder, and for nations it would stimulate cooperation instead of conflict and war.

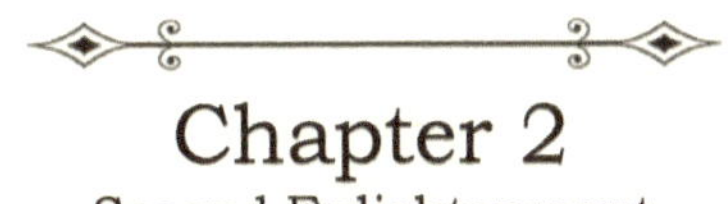

# Chapter 2
## Second Enlightenment

Today, once again major changes are occurring that shake the foundation of belief systems with their religious housing and impact on culture. People world-wide are recognizing for the first time that war and military force could destroy the world but continue to be necessary to solve global conflict and stop tyranny; that negotiation and cooperation are failing; that self -interests of political powers and economic networks are sacrificing individual well-being and widening the gap between rich and poor; that failure of schools to provide useful education is increasing; and finally that nature's ability to support human life is over taxed because of demands and abuses of increased population. Traditional sources of meaning, purpose, and guidance are being questioned and modified as occurred during the Axial Age and the Enlightenment explained in the preceding chapter. We may be in the advent of a second Axial Age or a second Enlightenment—a period of major changes in the institutionalized belief systems that have dominated societies and organized culture. There are currently many indications that major changes are occurring.

One indication of major change is a universal feeling of crisis. Fear of climate change is now world-wide. Also, around the world, governmental powers are being overthrown leading to drastic turmoil and hardship, particularly in the Middle East and Africa. The upsetting of dominating political powers has released shocking upheavals and violence. In the United States, dissatisfaction with the efficiency and cost of government services is calling for major changes. Traditional culture is undergoing change because of issues such as inequality, injustice, and racism. People are realizing that human existence is vulnerable, and that if changes in direction are not made, the exhaustion of our environment's ability to support our existence will be hastened and social competition will increase.

Another strong indication of major change is the upheaval in religious demographics. Recent polls in the United States indicate that about 90% of the population state belief in some form of supernatural deity that started the universe and may continue to exert influence; however, participation in traditional religious activities has dropped precipitously (PewForum, 2019). In between the fundamentalist believers and the atheistic deniers is a growing group known as "nones." These are people accepting a religious culture but denying association with beliefs of the traditional religions. Included are those saying they are spiritual but not religious.

Spirituality is a popular term for an attitude of concern about a transcendent realm signifying a meaning and purpose higher or better than those of merely meeting immediate physical needs. More about this is in Chapter 4, but important here is recognition of the increasing interest that there might be a transcendent realm and that dissatisfaction with dogmatic views of traditional religions is also increasing. Related to this is a resurgent interest in "big questions" concerning why we are here, how things got started, and where are we going (Wheeler, 2019). Now that we know so much about what is going on, we can use our knowledge in an attempt to make life more satisfying and the world more comfortable if we can reconcile the conflict between traditional religion, science, and modern experience.

Major change is also occurring in science. An example is the growing movement called Positive Psychology (Seligman, 2011) resulting from research in psychology, neuroscience, and interdisciplinary studies of history, sociology, anthropology, and medicine. This movement shifts efforts focused on pathology and disease to prevention and health. The term "flourishing" is used to support a philosophy of life that tolerates differences of opinion and social custom, and provides a purpose of striving for "eudaimonia," a feeling of satisfaction that one is thriving and that one's actions are contributing to the well-being of oneself and of society (Flanagan, 2009). This is more than just being happy. It means having a feeling of meaning for one's own life in the face of adversities and seemingly meaningless situations. It recognizes that there is much beyond our current knowledge, but that we must live in the world as it presents itself to us here and now with the knowledge we currently have. It preserves respect for the mysteries of existence without requiring non-logical explanations.

Major changes are causing upheavals in accepted attitudes and lifestyles. Adjusting traditional religious beliefs to be compatible with newfound knowledge may shake some faith, but by making beliefs more logical and less conflicting, the benefits of religion would be more available to both believers and non-believers. This means accepting a pluralism that allows other possible realities including a possible transcendent divine realm, and recognizing that although anything is possible, we must live in the world as it presents itself to us here and now. Such a foundation could be called "pragmatic pluralism," which is explained in Chapter 8 as having the potential for empowering people of faith, for enlightening the increasing number of unaffiliated spiritual seekers, and for encouraging those wanting more meaning and satisfaction in their lives.

Such a rejuvenation of culture and religion would restore the vitality, creativity, productiveness, and power that constitute the "American way of life," and produce an effective defense against threatening aggression. The resulting message will be not only inspiring and beneficent; it will also be helpful, informative, and sensible.

This is a great vision of the future. Civilization has steadily developed, and it will probably continue; however, it must be recognized that at the present time not all societies are in the same stage. There are still some societies and nations that use or support aggressive violence to pursue selfish goals. In these situations, only physical power is respected. Consequently, pacification, negotiation, and beneficence may need to lag behind use of military force. If a threat occurs and diplomacy is ineffective, military force should be used without hesitation, keeping in view long-range goals of peace, tolerance, respect, and progress.

Despite advances, there are clouds on the horizon. The nuclear age has brought massive capabilities that could destroy human life prematurely. Exploitation of natural resources and population increase could trigger a breakdown in availability of sustenance and upset the normal  support from our solar system. We may not have a billion years to work on surmounting physical limitations.

Science is moving from explanations of existence based on particles and forces to explanations based on fuzzy constituents such as information, consciousness, and intelligence, which are less vulnerable to future destruction. This is supported in Chapter 7. There are probably one billion years available for further changes to take place in human nature and for new forms of life to emerge. To achieve this, though, major changes in human nature must occur. The shifting base for values and faith is causing social upheavals, and acceptance of any major changes will be difficult. People must become oriented toward contributing to civilization's advancement; toward improving existence for all rather than focusing only on gratifications and selfish desires. The replacement of aggression, conflict, and extremism with cooperation, tolerance, and peace would not only reduce violent competition but would also make daily life more meaningful and manageable, and it would alleviate a major source of stress, anxiety, and depression. Furthermore, it may prevent human-made catastrophe and facilitate emergence of a form of life resistant to that ultimate global warming. Can we use the next billion years to continue development of life that will survive destruction of physical matter?

Major changes in religious activity indicate some positive trends. Several surveys and statistical analyses reported by organizations such as Gallop Poll, Pew Research Center, and Public Religion Research Institute are showing a major drop for belief in traditional religions and attendance in their activities. However, participation in non-traditional religious activities is increasing as are concerns about spirituality and God. The major cause of this shift has been associated with the recent publicity about research findings and personal experiences that raise questions about explanations and dogma provided by traditional religions. Major changes are occurring in religious beliefs throughout Western culture, and in the United States a number of quasi-religious organizations have developed such as Universal-Unitarian church, Ethical Society, and Religious Naturalism.

Religious Naturalism is a movement that grew out of the "Institute on Religion in An Age of Science" (IRAS) that attempts to respect the sacredness of nature while accepting research findings compatible with modern experiences. It considers nature as consisting of everything that exists, and that the term God represents the sacred depths of nature that inspire respect and awe. IRAS sponsors a web site for discussions and the journal *Zygon* that is a major publication of articles and research reports about religion-science issues. Contents and discussions have a pragmatic nature in that they concern basic current concerns of individuals and societies. It emphasizes a critical realism that recognizes that we do not really know the true nature of ultimate reality, but a universal task is to pursue more knowledge of it. There is room in this movement for a concern about the need to popularize this task, and to be open to various views of ultimate cause. This is a long-range goal that is often subjugated to more immediate goals of existence and is often pushed out of conscious concern. People tend to accept established beliefs about ultimate reality thus avoiding personal efforts of making beliefs more sensible and resolving conflicts. Furthermore, they tend to become so invested in a belief that they become intolerant of alternate views.

There seems to now be a shift from classic top-down religious dogma to a bottom-up induction of information that allows religion to incorporate findings of science and allows science to incorporate theories of religion. This recognizes the increased manageability and comfort in daily life provided by science, and the improved well-being and sense of meaning in life provided by religion. The result is the melding of knowledge, experience, and history into religions that is sensible and inspiring. It seems that we are in the midst of a major shift that could be called the "Second Reformation," similar to the Reformation that took place in sixteenth century Europe against the stifling dominance of the Roman Catholic hierarchy.

People in the United States are revolting not only against church dogma that conflicts with science and experience, but also against political control that limits freedom and creativity. This top-down to bottom-up shift is liberating the innate desire that we all have for a believable and understandable philosophy of our existence similar to the shift that occurred during the eighteenth century Enlightenment in Europe to undermine the dictatorial authority of church and government. A "Second Enlightenment" could be occurring.

Would it not be nice if governments, media, businesses, and religions were supporting this on-going developmental task instead of their current emphasis on political, economic, and ideological aggression and domination? The replacement of science-religion conflict with compatibility and tolerance would not only reduce violent competition but would also make daily life more manageable and alleviate a major source of anxiety and depression.

This is a noble challenge with such a long-range goal that it may be difficult to see its benefits, or it may be seen as a useless task. Most people are so busy with current activities meeting immediate daily needs that little time is available to think about several years into the future, let alone to think about a billion years from now. However, history shows that in all known ages respected leaders have voiced concern about explanation of existence, its source and purpose, and its future. It seems to be an innate characteristic of thinking humans that surfaces differently in different people, but it makes concern and explanation about the survival and purpose of life unavoidable. This innate concern could be called the ontological imperative.

# Chapter 3
## Ontological Imperative

A universal characteristic of normally thinking people is to wonder about why they are here, where they came from, and where they are going—the source, explanation, and meaning of existence. This is the primary or basic motivation that supplies fuel for daily activities. History indicates that ever since people have had the ability to be conscious of self, this underlying motivation has been a major concern and has supplied foundation for religions and many branches of science. In psychology the fields of existential (May, 1994), humanistic (Severin,1973), and positive (Seligman, 2011) psychologies have focused on this need through researchers such as William James (1906), Gordon Allport (1955), Viktor Frankl (1997), and Abraham Maslow (1971). More recently Robert Emmons (1999) has popularized the term "ultimate concerns," and shown its relationship to "personal strivings" and feelings of well-being.

Because the answers to these ultimate concerns are nebulous and difficult to think about, people tend to align themselves with established ideas and beliefs of other people, institutions, or organizations. Such belief systems have formed culture, created religions, and dominated societies. They range all the way from determinism established by a theistic force to materialism that excludes any determining force beyond observable nature. Psychology research shows that this wonderment creates an innate need that can be called "ontological imperative" (Wheeler, 2019).

Ontos is an ancient Greek word representing being as the fundamental aspect of existence. Ontology is the branch of philosophy that studies the ultimate being and ultimate reality that is the object of the ontological imperative. The use of the term ontos to represent the object of the ontological imperative avoids some of the problems associated with use of such terms as God, Creator, and Deity. The major problem with the currently used terms is their association with dogmatic beliefs that are now being questioned.

Even though the ontological imperative seems to be a universal human characteristic, it is manifest in many ways. For many people it is not as pressing as the needs of daily life such as job, food, and entertainment. The less pressing ultimate concerns get pushed into recesses of the subconscious mind where they create an unsettled feeling and may surface unexpectedly. For many people this concern is met by subscribing to answers provided by a belief system already established, one learned in childhood or through subsequent experience. These answers become socialized activities that in addition to meeting ultimate concerns, supply many other benefits such as group belongingness, social support, moral guidance, and acceptance. Even for people who accept those answers, though, an innate desire to learn more about the source and its nature usually lingers.

When a person is consciously concerned with this ontological imperative, two aspects become important.

First, what is the imperative? Is it to find a purpose in life or is it merely to have a goal or a hierarchy of goals? Is it to have a sense of purpose in one's own life, or for the purpose of life in general? Is it about me or about everybody? Much research is available about the role of an individual's sense of meaning in life (MIL) and purpose in life (PIL), particularly for their health, well-being, and performance (Hooker, Masters, & Park, 2017). The famous Austrian psychiatrist Viktor Frankl (1997), mentioned in the Introduction, dealt with this directly and helped set the stage for humanistic and positive psychology by developing a therapy aimed at helping people uncover their PIL. What they think it is does not matter, as long as they think that they have one. This is explained further in Chapters 11 and 12.

The second aspect of the ontological imperative is the nature of its goal, the goal's source, and the nature of that source—what is reality? Is it a divine force or great architect that designed and created our universe and gave purpose to life, or is it something else that started the evolution of complexity from fundamentals such as forces and fields to particles, then to matter, to life, and finally to humans? Modern science and philosophy have supplied support for many theories from theistic design to naturalistic evolution (Wheeler, 2019). Most scientists admit that at the present time, adequate explanation is not objectively known. The nature and source of ultimate reality is currently beyond the view of science and can only be revealed or speculated. Even the revealed answers of religions are now recognized as interpretations of human minds subject to private opinions. Objective explanation may even be forever beyond the grasp of human awareness. Whether ultimate reality is God, some other transcendent force, or a mysterious not yet discovered natural force, is not as important as recognizing the importance of its consideration for human well-being. More on this is in Chapter 6 which discusses views of reality.

In the meantime, a major useful aspect of the imperative's objective is the search for meaning, purpose, and explanation of existence. The study of this is what philosophy calls ontology but a more modern term is "ontosscience" to reflect a bottom-up scientific approach to the ontos as representing the object of ultimate concerns. (Ontos was defined previously as being, the fundamental aspect of existence.) This forms basic motivation, started by the ontological imperative, and the energizer of secondary motivations to meet immediate daily needs.

Despite our improved standard of living with its comforts and entertainment particularly in the United States, there are increasing rates of depression, anxiety, suicide, and criminality. Many people are dissatisfied and have a feeling of meaninglessness or discontent from wanting something more—something more than their daily struggles and the consumerism, crime, fraud, conflict, and terrorism they are bombarded with by the media. They want something more than politicians and community leaders that push for power and self-interests; something more from educators that cater to radical activists and teach self-enhancement and material wealth; and something more than nations that pursue warfare, global conflict, and violence. All of this is possible if pursuit of the ontological imperative is emphasized and more widely recognized.

Even though pursuit of the ontological imperative has not been popular recently, there are indications of renewed interest. There is a growing population that has broken away from traditional religion with its social structure of church, temple, mosque, etc. They are abandoning traditional activities but still desire spiritual activities (PewForum, 2019). Where traditional religions are declining, non-traditional religions and other related movements are growing and concerns about the ontological imperative are being renewed. The term "spirituality" captures the new interest, a concern about something beyond immediate physical existence. This is a desire for new approaches to ultimate concerns considering something beyond immediate experiences, a renewed pursuit of the ontological imperative.

# Chapter 4
## Spirituality

**M**ost people have at some time looked up in the sky on a clear night and wondered about the stars, the vast empty space, and what might lie beyond that which is visible. Is there something unknown beyond what is seen, containing something that might account for existence of such things as God, Deity, or extraterrestrial beings? The farther astronomers can look out in space, the more they see and also, the farther physicists can look into the atom, the more they see. The limits of outer space, the "macrocosm," studied by astronomers, and the limits of inner space, the "microcosm," studied by sub-atomic physicists expand with the increase in observational capabilities. This indicates that both outer and inner space extend beyond what is observable and may even be infinite or eternal (Ellis, 2011). A logical conclusion is that there is more than what is now known, maybe even reality beyond our comprehension. And this observation is made many times by people from their own experiences even when not aware of the sophisticated scientific findings and theorizing.

Research about attribution theory (Heider, 1944) supports a natural propensity for people to attribute cause for happenings and observations. What is the cause of the hardships and discomforts we struggle with on a daily basis? This extends to ultimate concerns such as the cause of existence, why are we here, what is the purpose of life? In attempting to provide answers to these deep questions, religions and cultural traditions have developed various beliefs. A common thread in these beliefs is a goal of transcending our current state of existence to accommodate some form of ultimate cause (more on this is in Chapter 5). Aldous Huxley (1944) captured this concern with his term, "perennial philosophy," a universal provision in most cultures to seek explanation of existence and to explore an ultimate cause.

Psychotherapist Carl Rogers (1961) popularized the theory that there must be something beyond our personal physical "life-space," and he showed the benefit of thinking outside of one's own life-space, to things beyond everyday experiences. Whether there is or is not a force beyond our life-space, people seem to have a need for such a belief, or at least a provision for such a possibility. Psychiatrist Robert Cloninger (2004) effectively supported "self-transcendence" as a personality characteristic that is a desire of people to reach out beyond themselves and "experience unity" with a mystical realm. Behavioral geneticist Dean Hamer (2004) has located activity in the brain indicating that even though existence may be a dominant concern, a desire to experience and understand esoteric self-transcendence is genetically based and inherent in our cognitive process. Neurobiologist Kevin Nelson (2011) and radiologist Andrew Newberg (2001) have independently drawn similar conclusions from their research about physiological brain activity associated with these experiences. Dr. Newberg (2010) has taken a brain-based concern with a mystical transcendent realm further supporting neurotheology, a neurological study of religious phenomena.

Science cannot do much about this mysterious realm because it is limited to observation of natural phenomena that is reliable, objectively supported, and independent of opinion or speculation. Religion on the other hand, does not have those constraints and provides explanation for these ultimate concerns by invoking the concept of supernatural powers. Religion dominates most cultures but recently its explanation has been brought into question by conflicts with research findings and modern experiences causing confusion in religion's reliance on a supernatural power.

Biochemist Stuart Kauffman in his bestselling book *Reinventing the Sacred* (2008) showed how a naturally occurring process of self-organization leads to a human complexity that gives rise to a sense of mysticism and sacredness without need for a supernatural power or a transcendent realm. Research about quantum theory has opened the door for non-material cause of our material environment independent of supernatural cause. Abrahamic religions (Judaism, Christianity, Islam) have difficulty dealing with these issues, although many related quasi-religious movements such as Ethical Society, Universal Unitarian Church, Theosophy, and Religious Naturalism recognize a sacredness arising from awe and mystery of nature without the constraints of traditional religious dogma (Goodenough, 1998). These movements are growing in popularity because of the many people who now report themselves as being spiritual but not religious.

All of these considerations are included in the term spirituality that is increasing in stature mainly because of growing dissatisfaction with traditional religion. Both religious dogma and its opposite, militant atheism, are being questioned. Spirituality is not constrained by either and allows other approaches to ultimate concerns. Much is now being published about spirituality; however, most is of esoteric or inspirational nature. The classic textbook *Psychology of Religion* by Spilka, Hood, Hunsberger, and Gorsuch (2003) devotes a few paragraphs in the first two chapters about spirituality being an aspect of religion, and in a later chapter about its role in mysticism; but little about it as a basic psychological characteristic in itself. More detailed information about the relationship of spirituality to religion has been presented in *The Handbook of the Psychology of Religion and Spirituality* (Paloutzian & Park, 2005) and *Psychology, Religion, and Spirituality* (Nelson, 2009), and the reader is referred to those compendiums for additional details and support. Although the information presented here is brief and selective, it is representative of reputable information and does not conflict with the more comprehensive reports of research results.

Spirituality has been defined and measured in many ways. One widely used measure focuses on seeking meaning, purpose, and transcendence (Ellison, 1983). Other measures were developed using standard statistical psychometric techniques focusing on characteristics independent of other personality factors and related to common aspects of leading spiritual traditions. Studies using these measures have supported spirituality as being an independent personality factor related to other established personality factors and spiritual activities (Rican & Janosova, 2010).

More directly, though, spirituality can be defined as an attitude of concern about something beyond daily experiences, something bigger and better than immediate current existence, a transcendent realm. As a personality characteristic, spirituality has been empirically related to mental and physical health and sense of well-being by several researchers (Vaillant, 2008). Some people are more conscious of this concern than others are; some accept a religious belief about a transcendent realm on faith; some set it completely aside; but throughout history, concern has been a major force. "Spiritual intelligence" which is the ability to recognize this concern and to effectively deal with it, has stimulated new research that validates this use of the term spirituality and has shown it to have beneficial effects (Emmons, 1999).

Since spirituality is an outgrowth of the ontological imperative, attempts to obtain replicable information about the validity and nature of spiritual phenomena could be called "ontological research," with "ontological engineering" being attempts to apply this information for the benefit of individuals and society. These are aspects of spirituality that combine science and religion and have the potential to provide beneficial relations within and between both individuals and societies that could replace the current competition for power and dominance with cooperation and helpfulness.

Despite tremendous capabilities of human intelligence, they are limited, and there is a tendency for individuals to latch on to the products of their personal experiences and fixate on them as reference points. However, questions about ultimate concerns continue, increasing interest in spirituality. One major question involves concern about the feeling people have for purpose and meaning in their lives. This is discussed in Chapters 11 and 12; however, it is useful here to recognize that the spirituality movement provides a useful way to explore such ultimate concerns. People want more than the currently popular view that the purpose of human life is only to exist and to further existence by developing what seems to be most useful here and now. Ramifications of this desire for more are limited only by the extent to which they are considered. Some of the purposes that have been objectively supported include self-enhancement, emergence, complexity development, actualization of potential, and flourishing. None of these require a transcendent deity; however, pursuit and fulfillment has been so difficult that most cultures have historically supported subjective conclusions from religion and philosophy about ultimate purposes such as doing God's will, unifying with a divine realm, or pursuing divine knowledge.

Most concepts about ultimate goals for human life are based on religious beliefs involving supernatural power, but spirituality is being supported by new considerations. Philosopher Owen Flanagan (2009) has made a commendable attempt to show that supernaturalism is not necessary with his concept of eudaimonistic flourishing. From his work with neuroscience, he concludes that meaning, spirituality, and transcendence are part of nature, and are best met by flourishing; that is, by living the "good life," experiencing beauty and awe, accepting ultimate explanations as possible myths, and gauging morality on mutual benefits. (This was already mentioned in Chapter 2 and is explored more in Chapter 11.)

Gordon Allport's (1955) concept of "religious sentiment" captures this concern about ultimate purpose as a cultural tendency that has been expanded to include "quest" emphasizing the search for a framework of belief supporting an ultimate reality (Batson, 1993). Most research about religious belief focuses on the content or end-product of belief as opposed to the search or seeking process. Seeking has been related to a lack of satisfaction in life, but the advantages of its pursuit overcome adverse effects (Newman, Schneider, & Stone; 2022). The pursuit increases tolerance of uncertainty and openness to new information and ideas while maintaining sufficient focus and faith to prevent unproductive confusion and vacillation. It is increasingly being recognized that spirituality is a natural ongoing striving process, a long-range seeking pursuit, a quest.

A notable attempt to support spirituality as an essential human striving for purpose and explanation of ultimate reality was the publication of *Spiritual Evolution* by the Harvard medical researcher and psychiatrist George Vaillant (2008). He has spent a career studying human development and health and pointed out how spirituality evolves as a stimulating process for positive emotions through three avenues: biologically over millions of years of brain development, culturally over thousands of years of social development, and individually over a person's lifetime of personal adjustment. Spirituality has become hardwired in the brain and through it people naturally generate positive emotions (Heid, 2021). The terms "ultimate concerns" and "ultimate reality" (Emmons, 1999) have become popular, and are being used along with other terms such as God, Truth, Creator, Deity, Light, and Word that are possible objects of the spirituality quest. Spirituality has become a force to open religious dogma to new information about these ultimate concerns.

There are many examples of current movements to open religions to ideas more compatible with scientific findings and modern experiences. One example is the recently popular book *A God That Could Be Real* by Nancy Adams (2015) who is the wife and colleague of astrophysicist Joel Primack. She summarized research about emergence which she defined as the creation of something new that is more than the sum of its parts. This occurs when complexity has increased to a critical point. She showed how spirituality emerged from the human mind as the brain complexity increased, and that the concept of God emerged from an increase in the popularity and complexity of spirituality. It seems that just as the mind emerged from the increased complexity of the brain, spirituality emerged as complexity of the mind increased, and that the deity/deities that dominated histories emerged from the increased complexity of spirituality.

Another example of a reputable system proposed to overcome dissatisfaction with the major traditional religions is panentheism that grew out of process theology. This has been explained by Philip Clayton and Stephen Knapp (2011) by viewing God as an ultimate cause, that people are a part of God, and that both are continuing to develop. Theistically oriented people that dislike questionable supernatural claims of religions are being attracted to such a belief system because it is more accommodating of research findings and more consistent with current personal experiences.

Some Christian apologists are developing ways to make religious dogma more compatible with experience and science. A good example of this is the work of the noted theologian Gordon Kaufman (2006) that calls for thinking of God not as the creator, but as the creativity that made possible the emergence and development of humans. This Creativity is not an explanation of the ultimate mystery of existence but is a descriptive term for the process. In his book, *Jesus and Creativity*, Dr Kaufman summarizes shortcomings in the dualistic picture of Jesus (material and divine) and emphasizes Jesus's teachings that were radical at that time. At the present time a new culture is needed based on Jesus's teachings to subdue instincts of self-preservation and self-defense with a spirit of self-sacrifice for improving the well-being of humanity. This does not negate Jesus's divinity but makes it a part of the ultimate mystery of creativity.

Even though use of the term spirituality seems new, it can be traced to ancient history. An example of the need to break away from religious constraints and reach for something more is the ancient movement of Freemasonry that traces its history to King Solomon three thousand years ago. It developed as a major organization after the Enlightenment when many people were attempting to shake the shackles of ecclesiastical dogma and political dominance that were creating hardships and subduing a sense of freedom and pursuit of advancement. It continues today as a major fraternal organization. Its only dogma is that there is a master Great Architect of the universe who exemplifies Truth. Truth is symbolized as the "Master's Word" and a major goal is attainment of knowledge about the Master's Word and what it stands for. "In the beginning was the Word and the Word was God" (Bible, 1976, John 1:1).

Freemasonry uses truth in two different ways. One as a tenet advocating honesty and correctness, and the other as ultimate reality symbolized by the Master's Word which has been lost and is the object of search. Because of the allusive nature of the ultimate nature of Truth, allegories and symbols with rituals and ceremonies are used that provide structure for abstract ideas making the pursuit enjoyable and meaningful. There are many interpretations about the meanings of the symbols and rituals providing a varied and tolerant approach to divinity. Even though these interpretations are varied because of an oral tradition, an authoritative summary was assembled by Albert Mackey (1921) in *An Encyclopedia of Freemasonry* that is still in use. The attraction of Freemasonry through the years is an example of the universality of spirituality and the attractions of associated activities such as comradery, fraternity, pageantry, and charity.

Although spirituality is proposed here as a universal human characteristic, it is manifest in many different ways resulting in many forms. In addition to the impact of varied experiential and social factors, genetic and biological mechanisms have been found to affect the spiritual activity of individuals. Despite the variance, these factors cause many people to be concerned about what is beyond immediate experience. Many times, the pressures of immediate daily existence over-ride spirituality concerns and create a conflict in efforts. Psychologist Rollo May (1967) described this conflict as the "human dilemma" which is a major source of anxiety that can be treated with psychological therapy. Since existence comes first, many people become bogged down in their own personal immediate needs, fears, desires, and pleasures to such an extent that they suppress their sophisticated mental abilities and avoid thinking about these abstract topics. As psychiatrist Erich Fromm (1947) explained with his concept of "existential dichotomy," we tend to subjugate our higher human creative abilities and needs in order to meet our animal needs resulting in an "existential dilemma," conflict between physical and intellectual needs. For Dr. Fromm, this is a major source of anxiety and other mental health problems, so recognizing "higher" needs is essential for good mental health.

It may be helpful to look at spirituality as existing on different levels using dimensions. Abraham Maslow (1968) proposed a widely used motivational structure based on a hierarchy of needs that ranged from "deficiency needs"—physical sustenance, security, social relations, and self-esteem—to "metaneeds" such as beauty, order, justice, and meaning. Any of these needs may exert a force on the individual and could be considered dimensions. However, Dr Maslow's theory emphasizes a requirement for lower level needs to be met before attention is given to higher needs and is therefore more a stage theory. Thought and action are often dominated by the deficiency needs because of the requirements of daily living and a person may get stuck in one stage. Even though filling metaneeds is blocked, those higher-level needs are stored in the unconscious mind where they can be experienced as a vague yearning for nebulous satisfaction. The term "dimension" is used here to avoid a qualitative judgment about levels or stages of development because dimensions coexist as opposed to being sequential (Anna Freud, 1965). One dimension does not have to be resolved for other ones to exert conscious concern.

Meeting the deficiency needs can be considered a first dimension of spirituality where concerns of ultimate meaning and metaneeds are dormant. Spirituality is also dormant because of dominance of deficiency needs. At any time, though, spirituality may become a conscious concern. When deficiency needs are met sufficiently that a person can devote more thought and activity to other needs, focus can be made on a second dimension involving metaneeds and on developing one's potential. Dr Maslow called this actualization which makes this second dimension "egocentric" (Wheeler, 2019).

The third dimension of spirituality involves making one's belief about this system of needs sensible and compatible with experience and knowledge. This is ontological research and could be considered "ontoscentric." Activity involves recognizing shortcomings in established belief systems and the conflicts between them and daily experience. Attempts are made to define concepts in concrete ways so that they make sense, can be adjusted, and used for the benefit of oneself and others. This is ontological engineering which could be considered "homocentric."

A fourth dimension involves recognition that our cognitive ability, understanding, and knowledge are limited and that there is a vast unknown that extends beyond the observable physical environment. This recognition may include an ultimate power that could be some form of nature not yet discovered by science or it may be an ultimate power in a transcendent supernatural realm, a deity. Even the famous theoretical physicist Albert Einstein recognized a superior intelligence or spirit that can reveal itself in the knowable world or be a divine force in an unknown world (Calaprice, 2005). Activity in this fourth dimension involves pursuing knowledge about an ultimate power, to contribute to that knowledge, and to help society benefit thereby. Pursuit requires not only dedicated spirituality but also creativity, charisma, and a variety of abilities. It requires an awareness of the ontological imperative and thinking that is open to new ideas.

Dimensions 2, 3, and 4 involve activities that Maslow referred to as actualizing. He also supported a difference between nontranscendent and transcendent actualizers in writings published in 1971. The difference is that where nontranscendent actualizers are focused on achieving personal potentials, transcendent actualizers are focused on potentials beyond the self, to something bigger and higher.

Despite our society's dominance with dimension 1, the others exert a force that may be out of conscious awareness, stored in the subconscious mind, but can emerge into conscious concern at any time. The large percentage of the US population that support established religions are focusing on dimensions 1 and 2 because participation in their activities help meet both deficiency needs and metaneeds by using an established belief system and accepting that system's application and meaning. For many people participating in religious activities also involves dimension 3 by seeking spiritual knowledge and helping others. Also in dimension 3 are the growing number of people considered spiritual but not religious. They avoid the dogma of traditional religion in seeking spiritual information but are seeking spiritual knowledge.

The conceptualization, development, and pursuit of transcendent needs dominate dimension 4 activities. For people focusing on dimension 4, the underlying ideas (ideation) override worship and faith, and the mechanisms of religious practice become flexible and even superficial. These are the people that can enjoy religious ceremony and ritual but see them as vehicles for experiencing deep meaning. It seems that people investing to some degree in all dimensions have greatest well-being, but the investment in activity and processing seem to be much more important than success or the end-product.

This proposed structure of spirituality is consistent with results of extensive research by Lawrence Kohlberg (1984) about moral development and James Fowler (1981) about religious faith development, except that their structures are based on sequential stages rather than dimensions.

There are many theories about stages and dimensions of moral and spiritual development that lead to a high-level ultimate stage. A person may be aware of this ultimate level, and that awareness may make concern about that level over-ride concern about physical needs or other prior sequential stages (Wheeler, 2021). Worldly activities lose their dominating importance and are supplemented with focus on ultimate concerns.

Spirituality may lie dormant in one person and be a dominating activity in another person, but it is inherent in all either consciously or subconsciously and is an unavoidable force behind development of religious types of belief systems. All dimensions and systems of stages exist in a person, but the degree to which they are manifested is quite varied and people tend to focus on a particular dimension or stage.

Spirituality can be summarized as an attitude of concern about something bigger, higher, and transcendent to our daily activities to meet immediate needs. It is a natural outgrowth of the ontological imperative. The object of concern, the "something" is more than what we experience in daily lives, something that can be counted on as being true and real. Whatever it is, we are doomed to search for this "something." Being aware of this concern is a first step in feeling that life is satisfying and has purpose. The second step is activity in pursuit of the "something" that supplies purpose and meaning for existence. And the third step is experiencing satisfaction from a sense of personal development and contribution to humanity.

Despite the new interest in spirituality and increasing recognition of the ontological imperative, few people currently put effort in actions to pursue meaning and ultimate types of concern. It is too far out to be of immediate concern. There have always been speculative mystical movements such as spiritualism and psychism that have been concerned with otherworldliness, a mystical realm of spirits, ghosts, and goblins. These have been traditionally treated with disrespect by scientific researchers; however, recently some more reputable movements have developed that indicate possible validity of such a realm beyond our current physical environment, transcendent to our physical existence. This relates to an aspect of the new interest in spirituality—concern about the possibility of human life transcendent to currently known nature. Transcendence to a more comfortable realm was a major goal for our ancestors.

# Chapter 5
## Transcendence

Where spirituality is a concern about something beyond current environment, transcendence is the process of moving into a realm beyond current environment. Ever since Enoch translated from life directly into heaven during early biblical times because he "walked with" God (Bible, Hebrews 11:5, 1976), people have considered transcending their earthly existence for something more, an escape from the difficulties of life or a reach for something bigger, better, or more meaningful than their current existence. If everyone would consider transcendence now, many of the problems of today would be alleviated and possibly foster development of a form of life that will continue when material life on earth ceases as predicted in Chapter 1. The only problem with this is that since Enoch's time people have had difficulty "walking with God" sufficiently to be able to experience this way of transcending earthly existence, and unfortunately, people are decreasing in their ability for "walking with God."

Throughout known history humans have been concerned with the possibility of escaping from their immediate existence and transcending or moving to a more desirable realm. Life is tough. In earlier days it was much less secure and comfortable than it is now and the possibility of a better existence in some form of heaven was very comforting. Despite the technological advances, enjoyments, and comforts available in present times, our current existence has not provided an advanced level of well-being, and a sense of dissatisfaction is rampant (PewForum, 2019). In the past, various forms of metaphysical belief and religion supplied possible escape and justification for the discomfort. Conflicts between traditional beliefs and modern experiences are causing such questioning of traditional beliefs that their earlier benefits have now decreased. The current increase in dissatisfaction, anxiety, depression, crime, violence, and terrorism has been attributed to this loss of traditional beliefs; thus, supplying one explanation for renewed interest in transcendence (Kauffman, 2008).

Transcendence is defined as the quality or state of being beyond comprehension, beyond material existence (Merriam-Webster, 2008). It grows out of the ontological imperative discussed in Chapter 3, and may even have a biological base (Pearce, 2002). If this transcendence were possible, the continuance of life would be ensured. And, as pointed out in Chapter 2, even though such life continuance is a "long-shot," some progress is currently underway.

Developments about artificial intelligence are showing the feasibility of a computerized entity that far exceeds current human abilities and may surpass human limitations. The Transhuman movement is using medical advances in gene editing and body modification aimed at producing a "superhuman" that may surpass current limitations (Tirosh-Samuelson, 2012). And the Psychotronic Association is bridging research about science, spirit, mind, and technology to explore human potential. Such efforts have enough of a possibility to produce a new emergent form of life surpassing current limitations to receive funding support. However, there are physical and moral dangers in these efforts of "tinkering with life" and "playing God," but even theologians are supporting similar efforts (Weissenbacher, 2018).

A recent issue of the journal *Theology &Science* (*16(3), 2018)* was devoted to articles about human progress toward a transcendent state known as deification, sanctification, or divination with the question of appropriateness of human intervention. Information presented there supported a theory that the purpose of life is to grow and develop both as individuals and as a species. This is similar to the philosophy popularized by the famous French Jesuit priest, geologist, and paleontologist Teilhard de Chardin (1965) involving the "omega point" to which life is oriented. At that point human consciousness would be able to survive the eschaton (cessation of earthly existence) predicted by many religions and by the science of global warming (earth destruction by the sun). Chardin is not clear about the appropriateness of human interventions, nor is he clear if this can occur before material life is destroyed.

Many of the writers in the *Theology & Science* issue indicated this development is God's intention. Irenaeus, a famous Greek philosopher, established an early Christian position in the second century CE when he advocated that God created the universe so that a living organism would evolve naturally by overcoming the problems of material existence and meeting the challenges of evil using their own ingenuity.

The respected English physicist and theologian, John Polkinghorne (2007), proposed that our Creator's purpose was two stepped. First is the current human creation existing at some distance from an obscure "veiled" Creator so that creatures will have the freedom to make themselves without divine interference, and then the second step is the human creature's encounter with the "unveiled" riches of the divine creator's nature (having direct contact with God). He goes further to say that it is possible that God could create a form of matter not subject to the decay characterizing material of this world. Most religions provide for a non-material realm where personal consciousness continues after bodily death and can continue in places such as Heaven, Nirvana, and Jannah.

How comforting it is to think that such catastrophe can have a positive outcome. Most religions include a belief in such transcendence and advocate ways of achieving it. Success has always been allusive and limited to psychological or psychic experiences. It was the famous psychologist Abraham Maslow (1971) that popularized the term transcendence. But this was more scientifically based than was the religious or spiritual approach.

Dr Maslow's first major use of the term transcendence was in a 1960 lecture that was published by the *Journal of Humanistic Psychology* about good health resulting from transcendence of physical environment (Maslow, 1968). Here he advocated going beyond theories of motivation based on adjustment to theories based on thinking independently of the immediate environment and moving to something beyond or higher. He later wrote an article that was published posthumously showing that the healthiest people he studied not only thought about what he called meta-needs like beauty, harmony, and justice, but focused beyond the self, transcending immediate personal needs. Being able to focus on these high-level meta-needs he called actualization and those who were able to focus on these needs beyond the personal self, he called transcendent actualizers (Maslow, 1971).

In the 1971 book, Dr. Maslow gave thirty-five definitions of transcendence. All but two are concerned focusing on actions and considerations beyond the self and needs of immediate daily existence involving such things as transcendence of time, ego, superego, fear, conflicts, and current culture. These definitions provide support for the secondary theme of this book mentioned in the introduction which is to redirect the current emphasis on comfort, entertainment, and wealth to longer-range things such as development, explanation, and contribution. Such change in thinking would alleviate major currently increasing problems of anxiety, depression, suicide, crime, violence, and conflict. But the major theme of this book is the need for development of a form of life that can survive the inevitable destruction of physical nature on earth. This major theme is supported by Maslow's 23d definition of transcendence: "...to become divine or godlike, to go beyond the merely human." (p. 274); and by his 34th definition: "...transcendence of human limits...in which one can be an end, a god, a perfection..." (p. 278).

Psychologist Scott Kaufman (2020) who has carefully reviewed all of Maslow's writings concluded that those views of transcendence are associated with successful psychotherapy and improvement in social well-being, and are supported by his own clinical experience and research. Furthermore, Kaufman shows congruence with other notable psychological theories such as Jane Loevenger's theory of integrated ego development, and Erik Erikson's theory of psychosocial development. "It's time for us to take responsibility for the society we live in and to help create the conditions that will help all people to not only self-actualize but also to transcend." (p. 233).

Attempting to transcend one's current situation either to reach a higher level of functioning that is an aspect of natural reality, or to transition into an alternate reality raises the question of the nature of reality. Is there a reality to which we might transcend that is different from that which is currently observable? Is reality only what we make it, the result of our perceptions and thinking, or the result of meeting our needs for existence? Is reality an outgrowth of the transcendence desire, or of the ontological imperative seeking explanation of existence? Is there a universal reality underlying the various explanations of our observable environment? What is true and the foundation of "all that is"? What can we "hang our hats on?" Addressing these questions involves the deep thinking recommended in this book.

# Chapter 6
## Reality

Reality is formally defined as the quality of being real, fixed, permanent, or immovable. It is what we can count on as being true (Merriam-Webster, 2004). The object of the ontological imperative is to understand the reality underlying our existence. Is there a reality that is the source of our existence? Is there a reason for our existence? Did God or some other divine type of power start and maybe still influence life? Is our universe just one of many universes or alternate realities? Is what science knows about our universe all there is to reality? These perennial questions have dominated history and driven the development of civilization and culture forming the bases for religions and ideologies that continue today.

Because of the success of those religions and ideologies in providing comforts, entertainment, and technologies, it is no longer popular to think about these deep questions, about the reality underneath our world. Just use things if they work. But civilization is now in turmoil. Crime, violence, terrorism, mental illness, and global destruction are increasing, while sense of satisfaction and well-being are decreasing (PewForum, 2019). We need to think once again about the source of our existence, the nature of reality, what important is going on, and what is reality. If reality is the result of a divine power, we should do a better job of cooperating with it. If there is no divine power, we need to do a better job of figuring out and enforcing ethical social norms and standards of behavior.

Because of our uniquely human thinking ability, we naturally formulate ideas about the unknown. Since science cannot answer these ultimate questions, we resort to speculation. There must be a "first cause," a reality out there somewhere. There must be a moral authority out there whose judgements are more just than those of vacillating humans. There must be out there somewhere an object worthy of our devotion and worship. There must be a source for the creative process that develops and advances us individually and collectively.

Because our knowledge and thinking are limited, we usually adopt the assumptions already developed and accepted in our social environment. These assumptions evolved because they ameliorated concerns about reality, met needs, and improved society. But these assumptions formed dogmatic beliefs that had to be accepted on faith in a transcendent source, something metaphysical or supernatural. In Western culture God has become a catch-all term for this source, however sometimes more descriptive terms are used such as *Great Unknown, Master Spirit, Great Architect, Great I Am, or Creative Force.* To be more meaningful, symbols and other representations are adopted. Anthropomorphic is a term applied to representing God with human characteristics that we can more easily understand. God incarnate in Jesus is more meaningful than God as the Great I Am. Jesus, Mohammad, or Buddha are more effective objects of worship than abstract Spirits. So, it is not surprising that symbols and icons take on divine powers that conflict with scientific findings and modern experiences. The trade-offs become major issues. Which is better: belief in a reality that can be conceptualized with certainty and fills needs but conflicts with objective knowledge and modern experiences, or belief in a reality that is consistent with objective knowledge and modern experiences but are currently beyond understanding and subject to uncertainty and continual revision?

The first part of the book *Climbing Higher* (Wheeler, 2019) presents explanation of reality as an innate human need. Then four categories of reality views are developed. The most common view, "personal reality" is our personally accepted opinion and belief that varies among societies and individuals. It is usually a personal interpretation of a view learned in childhood. Since personal reality is known to be variable and subject to controversy, the question of a universal or ultimate reality is raised. The possibility of a "universal reality" that may have a divine type of power is the basis of most religions and has been important in the advance of civilization. Recent scientific findings and modern personal experiences have created big questions about a universal reality that has shaken the foundations of traditional religions.

A third view of reality grew out of the need to account for the occurrence of bad things such as World War I and II and how they can be prevented. This is "existential reality" which faces the good and bad experiences in everyday life for which we must take responsibility and actively manage.

A fourth view is "pragmatic reality" which is how we deal with immediate daily situations here and now despite personal views, beliefs, and difficulties. This is recognition that effectively managing daily activities may be more important than theorizing about reality.

All views may be valid. We do not really know. There may be a mysterious realm with a transcendent intelligence that empowers our existence, but despite the comfort of faith, it is helpful to shoulder responsibility for the outcome of personal activities without depending on help from a transcendent power. We best live in the world as it presents itself to us here and now and strive for sustenance while also pursuing advancement and explanation of existence. Living in the here and now while also pursuing ultimate concerns would facilitate a constructive meaning and sense of purpose to our activities.

How to know reality has been a perennial issue that developed the philosophy of epistemology, study of the nature, origin, and scope of knowledge and how we know what we know. There is a question of whether it is possible to know reality or even if there is such a thing. The respected contemporary philosopher David Chalmers insists in *Reality+* (2022) that we may exist in a virtual reality that may be a simulation created by an unknown force that could be called God. In any case, though, for day-to-day functioning we all need to have a feeling that there is a consistency in our environment that enables continuing management of needs and activities.

A topic pertaining to reality has recently developed involving basic constituents of matter, our material environment. As physicists investigate sub-atomic particles new questions arise about the underlying reality. Physicists have now peered into the atom far enough to determine that the most basic constituents seem to be fields and forces that can relate to immaterial constituents such as information, intelligence, consciousness, and spirit that get close to dealing with the fundamental first cause of universal reality. This view of basic constituents relates both supernatural and natural approaches to reality and supplies explanation for some previously unexplained phenomena.

# Chapter 7
## Basic Constituents

Amazing advances in science have occurred because of reductionism, breaking things down into underlying parts, constituent parts. As scientists can look farther inside the atom, more constituents are found. At the most fundamental level, there seems to be a common fundamental constituent (FC).

This is scientifically supported in the materialism approach to reality of theoretical physics and various branches of sub-atomic science. Constituents such as strings, vibrations, fields, forces, and energy have been discovered that in turn seem to have a more fundamental constituent still being looked for. This ultimate FC has been supported by indirect observation and theorized to be something like information, consciousness, intelligence, zero-point energy, hyper-dimension, etc. (Kuhlmann, 2013). The nature of this type of FC is appreciated in the materialistic approach because matter is recognized as mainly fuzzy space having forces that create the hard surfaces we feel as physical material. The particles that have been detected in atoms are created by these forces and seem to consist of nebulous things that could also be based on an ultimate FC yet to be found in nature. Or it may be something beyond nature associated with an unknown alternate reality. Recently proposed theories of Multiverse and Many

Worlds support alternate realities where unknown worlds could exist with different forms of matter and different FCs (Haisch, 2010; Wheeler, 2019).

The approach to reality of theism proposed by religion supports an FC that is easiest to grasp, best defined, and most popular; however, it results from subjective experience and has the least scientific support. Because we live in a "cause and effect" environment and have such a strong need for a "first cause," various forms of a supernatural deity have developed such as God, Allah, and Brahmin. Belief in such deity effectively provides for an FC that is easy to grasp and has been the basis for religions and ideologies that still dominate societies despite conflicts with recent research findings and modern experiences. Advantages, disadvantages, and importance of religion were discussed in the previous chapter and in Chapter 1.

In between the materialistic and theistic approaches to reality is idealism supported by recent studies indicating that the FC underlying our universe is some form of mental activity such as consciousness that exists as a universal "cosmic force," and from which the material world developed (Robinson, 2020). The personal consciousness of an individual could be an aspect of that universal consciousness. The idealistic approach has support from quantum physics where our material environment results from the coalescence or collapse of potentialities (Polkinghorne, 2007). This approach is also supported in psychology with research about psychic phenomena and psi energy resulting from an unknown type of mental force (Radin, 2013). The term consciousness has been broadened to stand for more than just human awareness. It seems reasonable that a form or aspect of a universal consciousness could carry over to personal human consciousness (Rue, 2006). There is even support from information technology for a human's personal consciousness to be related to a primal universal consciousness and thus be an aspect of a cosmic consciousness (Lohrey 2018).

The conflict between materialism and idealism was resolved in the seventeenth century when Rene Descartes organized the philosophy of dualism. This is the theory that both mental and material nature exist separately. But dualism also has problems explaining scientific observations, and recently the philosophy of panpsychism has been recalled in various forms to solve the problems associated with material, theistic, idealistic. and dualistic approaches.

Panpsychicism proposes that consciousness is not only the FC but is present in everything. The contemporary philosopher Philip Goff has modified panpsychism and built a reputable case for consciousness to be an FC but not everything is conscious. Consciousness resides as the FC in the basic components that make up everything. In *Galileo's Error* (2019), Dr Goff also points out the feasibility of an unknown "third element" that could replace consciousness as the FC. Several other similar theories have been proposed forming a version of panpsychism called panprotopsychism. These theories support an FC from which consciousness emerges called protoconsciousness (Goff, Seager, Allen-Hermanson; 2022). This is not a new idea. Neutral monism was proposed by the famous British psychologist and philosopher Bertrand Russell in

1927 as the theory that there was a third element underlying both the mental and material elements of dualism (Russell, 2009). Establishing a third element term would be useful by eliminating confusion with the consciousness term and allow consciousness to revert to its traditional role representing mental awareness. This would recognize that the nature of an FC is not known at the present time even though its existence is indicated through indirect observation.

Each of the four approaches to reality emerged from experiences, observations, and need for explanation. Each has a way of explaining many mysterious phenomena. Each developed terms for an FC, but none are widely accepted, and they have nebulous meanings with conflicting background information. A term unencumbered by nebulous meanings is needed. Protoconscousness might be one. One might be Ontos, the ancient Greek word for fundamental being that was introduced in Chapter 3. Other candidates are: Zero Point, Preon, Aether, Is, More, It, and Creativity. Replacing the term consciousness as the FCs is a big jump similar to replacing the perception of the chair I am sitting on as being solid enough to support my body to viewing the chair as consisting of nebulous forces and fields. However, if you can believe what scientists say, you can think that it is possible, and you can feel that at the most fundamental level there is some kind of non-material-like constituent yet to be uncovered.

Science has now established a Periodic Chart of 112 elements, each of which is made up of eighteen different particles called fermions and five forces called bosons (Powell, 2018), referred to as the Standard Model. The particles have all been found to be made up of six types of quarks and leptons. As capabilities of nuclear science increased, constituents of quarks and leptons have been discovered that seem to be nebulous things similar to fields, vibrations, or maybe bundles of properties (Kuhlmann, 2013). Fields are best explained as some form of energy, and scientists are now searching for the nature of this basic form of energy.

Quantum theory supports exotic terms such as sygons (Hardy, 2016), psychons (DeBiase, 2009), and noetic fields (Amoroso & Martin, 2002). Such descriptions of energy fields are similar to metaphysical terms used in religions such as spirits, angels, and ghosts. Theoretical physicists have recently used preon as a general term that implies a common constituent, the leading candidate for which is a vibrating string (Lincoln, 2012). But what is vibrating? Before "string theory" was organized, the emanant physicist John Wheeler (1997) proposed it was information and there is now a sizable following supporting "information theory." The nature of this information is rather fuzzy and can be related to religion's use of "word" and "light." "In the beginning was the Word and the Word was God" (Bible, 1976, John 1:1). "And God said, let there be light: and there was light" (Bible, 1976, Genesis 1:3).

Consciousness is currently a widely used term to describe the FC, the fundamental constituent of matter. Traditionally consciousness has been considered a product of the brain, a mental awareness of the environment including awareness of oneself and one's own thinking process. Much is known about what this consciousness does, its levels and states. Attempts to explain how it occurs and how it produces mental results have resulted in broadened use of the term. One explanation previously explained sees a person's consciousness as an aspect of a universal or cosmic consciousness with which it can interact. It can also interact with other personal consciousnesses (Goff, 2019).

Quantum mechanics and quantum theory have supplied scientifically based support for consciousness as a "quantum mind" that collapsed or materialized "potentialities" forming our material environment (Walker, 2000). This aspect of consciousness could explain mysterious functions such as telepathy, psychokinesis, and insight (Radin, 2013). Thus, consciousness representing some form of mental force could be a basic constituent of fermions, those fundamental particles in the standard model. This concept is not really new. Most ancient religions incorporated a quantum type of mind with such things as Spirit, Holy Ghost, Atman, God, Brahman, Allah, etc. that represented an FC.

It is interesting that the terms being used in physics to explain ultimate constituents of matter are now overlapping with terms that have been used in metaphysics to explain religious beliefs. Is a melding taking place between these fields to explain the makeup of matter? As supernaturalism is needed to answer questions inaccessible to naturalism, metaphysics seems needed to answer questions inaccessible to physics. The divide between science and religion is decreasing and compatible views of reality are increasing even though religion is based on accepting explanation whereas science is based on doubting explanations. A paradox is that both are needed.

How can we have both? And how can we manage meeting our day-to-day needs and also pursue answers to long-range idealistic questions? How can we contribute to the survival of life pursuing the ontological imperative with its abstract spiritual needs and also pursue a view of reality useful in meeting needs of daily sustenance? For answers, a reorientation is needed of the current self-centered goals dominating society. It would be oriented to recognizing a need for something beyond materialistic daily activities, recognizing that we do not really know what that something is, and that we are destined to search for it while recognizing that anything is possible but that we must live in the here and now with what is probable. This is a worldview or philosophy-of-life that could be called Pragmatic Pluralism.

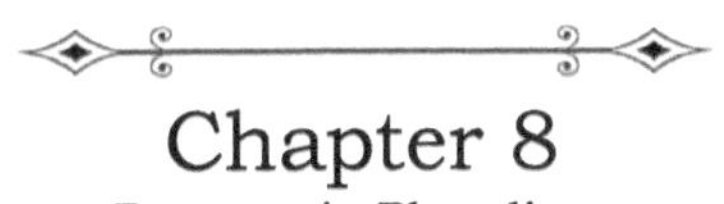

# Chapter 8
## Pragmatic Pluralism

A study of history and anthropology indicates that as far back as humans can be traced, they have had beliefs in supernatural powers. These beliefs grew out of the built-in need for explanation of existence—the ontological imperative introduced in Chapter 2. And these beliefs have been important in the development of civilization. Furthermore, studies of psychology, sociology, and neuroscience indicates that belief in supernatural power helps meet many important human needs such as meaning, purpose, social support, coherence, structure, acceptance, stable ethics, moral authority, and immortality. Anthropology and history show that such beliefs could have developed through adaptive evolution or could have been implanted by design (Szocik, 2017). Probably more important, though, are studies of recent findings from the physical sciences showing that explanations of our universe and existence support theories such as many-worlds, cyclic-universe, multiverse, cosmic-consciousness, and intelligent-design (Stephen, 2021). This implies scientific support and natural explanation for many mystical phenomena that had been attributed to a supernatural realm in the past.

The popular theories of quantum mechanics developed in physics nicely explain observations of subatomic activity where particles are also waves or forces that can exist in more than one place at the same time (superposition), that exist as multiple potentialities in a wave function until materialized (collapsed) by being observed or used, and once connected with another particle can communicate instantly (entangled) when separated from that once connected particle. Quantum mechanics opened the door for many interesting studies involving such things as consciousness and information being fundamental constituents of nature (discussed in the previous chapter).

Other interesting studies using recent scientific findings include the use of discoveries in physics by astrophysicist Bernard Haisch (2010) to support an information system that is an intelligence underlying the universe, a form of consciousness or "great thought" that created reality. Physicist Evan Walker (2000, p. 326) proposed that our material universe results from the realization or collapse of potentialities by a prehuman "quantum mind." He writes, "In the beginning was the Quantum Mind, a first cause, itself time independent and nonlocal, which created space-time and matter-energy." This could be called Supermind or even God as the Great Architect or Great Observer that not only started things but can intercede now at a quantum level. Thus, God could affect matter without violating physical laws.

The word atom comes from a Greek word meaning indivisible. Less than a hundred years ago the atom was considered the smallest object in nature. It could not be further reduced. However, as researchers peered into the nature of atoms and developed techniques for looking closer into their structure (microcosm), more was observed. Eventually atoms were found to be made up of sophisticated classes of particles and forces called fermions and bosons such as quarks, leptons, photons, and gluons. Furthermore, it seems that these basic particles and forces consist of energy that in turn consist of something more basic such as relationships, information, or intelligence (Kuhlmann, 2013). As discussed in Chapter 7, research continues to find other particles and forces indicating that there is still more to be found. The variety of subatomic constituents are limited only by the ability to observe them or their effects.

Similar results occur for the researchers that study outer space (macrocosm), in that the limits of space are a function of the distance that can be observed. Albert Einstein explained the observed limits of space as the result of space curving back onto itself. These limits have now been expanded to include dark matter, dark energy, and black holes with the possibility of  boundless reality and multiple universes. We exist in the universe that happens to have conditions that support our form of life (Davies, 2008). In other universes there may be different forms of life and different laws of nature—alternate realities.

Since the limits of the microcosm and the macrocosm expand with the expansion of observational capabilities, a logical conclusion can be made that space, nature, and time go on and on, maybe even to infinity. The concept of infinity is difficult to grasp, because within the realm of infinity not only could anything exist, but somewhere everything would exist. This would include unknown forces, spirits, souls, and deities that may exist in alternate realities as well as in unknown aspects of our natural reality. This implies a pluralism of realities beyond our known physical world, beyond the popular dualism of physical-mental. Such pluralism implies that unknown things may exist in our natural reality as well as in other possible alternate realities. Anything is therefore possible, even the Gods of our forefathers.

But in the meantime, we exist in a physical world whose nature we can know best through our sensory perceptions that are influenced by expectations, wishes, and beliefs that many times distort our view. Our uniquely human emotions produce feelings both good and bad that sometimes provide experiences with fleeting glimpses of an unknown realm, a realm indicating existence of a possible alternate reality with an environment different (metaphysical) or beyond (supernatural) our own. Unfortunately, these experiences are too ephemeral for practical use and reliable benefit. Greatest well-being seems to result from objective attempts to harness and use our known physical environment while pursuing metaphysical possibilities—striving to know the unknown while effectively using what is known.

This is where pragmatism enters. Even though anything is possible, we must live with what is happening here and now and with our view of what will probably occur. What is useful and practical comes best by being respectful of the unknown while living effectively with what is known. Such efforts have the probability of supplying an uplifting sense of meaning and purpose that energizes our daily struggles for immediate needs. It is important that we recognize useful reliable information about our situation and use it to live effectively in the "here and now" without suppression from unyielding ideology, or the sacrifice of personal belief, or of being diverted by speculation of possibilities and fear of uncertainty.

The term "pragmatic pluralism" has been used loosely over the years by philosophers trying to explain varied human perspectives on value, ethics, and religion that were originally proposed by William James (2006). This is explained by the notable Finnish philosopher Sami Pihlstrom in his 2013 book, *Pragmatic Pluralism and the Problem of God*. My book, *Mountains and Minds* (Wheeler, 2010) established a formal definition of pragmatic pluralism as a practical theory of life that recognizes the possibility of alternate realities while living effectively in the world as it now presents itself. This theory was supported in *Mountains and Minds* with what was considered scientific information and it was proposed as a foundation for a religious belief that makes sense with personal experience, and reliable information.

Pragmatic pluralism as proposed here is an alternative to theism that requires unquestioned faith in religious dogma and belief in a certain supernatural deity. It is also an alternative to atheism that is belief that there can be no supernatural deity, and as an alternative to agnosticism that believes there may be a supernatural deity but it is unknowable. As thusly defined, pragmatic pluralism admits that the "if and what" of deity is currently inconclusive but is accessible with further pursuit. Belief in some form of deity is useful, and with further development, questionable and uncertain aspects will decrease. If societies were oriented toward a joint pursuit of such development instead of competing for ideologically based dominance, much violence and terrorism would be replaced with cooperation and tolerance.

Pragmatic pluralism is a philosophy of life or worldview recognizing that anything is possible, but that not everything is probable and that it is best to live in the "here and now" as the world presents itself while pursuing knowledge of the mysterious unknown. It supports a belief in something transcendent to our personal self that supplies meaning and purpose for our existence, and that since we are uncertain of its nature, we are destined to search for knowledge of it and tolerate alternate views. Because of varied make-up and experience, we all have varied ideas about a philosophy of life or worldview and live with interpretations most useful and sensible to us individually. Pragmatic pluralism fits in with science, experience, and religion—it is a believable belief that could rejuvenate the benefits of religion.

Much anxiety, depression, and confusion would be reduced if people were more aware of the pragmatic pluralism philosophy, and if society emphasized it in addition to the current emphasis on material resources, comfort, and entertainment. Current feelings of dissatisfaction and lack of energy to meet demands of daily needs would be replenished with the realization that pursuing the ontological imperative is a basic motivation that supplies energy for secondary motivations to meet immediate daily needs.

# Chapter 9
## Motivation

Sometimes it is difficult to get out of bed in the morning, stumble through getting dressed, and trundle off to work. Sometimes challenges at work or other difficulties make you wonder why you are putting up with these hardships. Top on the list of reasons is money—we all need it. Then comes health followed by comfort, entertainment, relationships, and security. These are mainly physical and social needs, but is there something more? Study of needs, drives, desires, and reinforcements have been useful in explaining many needs and behaviors of living things, but for humans more is needed. The development of the human species and civilization indicates a pattern involving goals beyond just meeting immediate daily needs, something more that makes these efforts meaningful and worthwhile.

Never in the annals of human history have physical needs been better fulfilled. Lifespan has doubled in the past couple of hundred years and quality of health is vastly improved. Technology has provided control of personal climate, food abundance, and other sources for unparalleled comfort. Even entertainment is now widely available. Yet on the other hand, crime and murder has increased, and competition has become aggressive and many times violent. Mental health problems such as depression, anxiety, and anomie as well as suicide and domestic violence have mushroomed. A general mood of dissatisfaction is widespread (PewForum, 2019). With the astounding advances in civilization, why have there not been advances in sense of well-being and satisfaction? The answer lies somewhere in "something more," something more than meeting immediate daily physical needs, something more than the competition, consumerism, violence, and gratifications the media bombards us with and is emphasized be our leaders, politicians, and educators.

Research about human motivation has typically involved studies about meeting basic needs and desires such as money, job performance, health, comfort, sex, and security. During its hey-day in the middle 1900's, the psychology of motivation focused on rewards, reinforcements, and punishments. Studies of animal behavior explained much of what humans do, but much was still unexplained. The humanistic movement in psychology attempted to explain the higher-level human needs. A popular application to job performance were theories X and Y developed by Douglas McGregor (2006) using ideas from Abraham Maslow's hierarchy of needs (1968) introduced in Chapter 4.

Maslow's theory proposed that physical sustenance, security, belongingness, and self-esteem needs were basic to higher level actualization and metaneeds such as harmony, justice, beauty, and self-fulfillment. Theory X treated employees as needing close supervision with tangible rewards and immediate incentives in order to meet the basic needs. Theory Y treated employees as creative partners desiring to improve their performance and achieve the higher-level needs. These theories grew from the humanistic approach to psychology of researchers such as William James (2006), Gordon Allport (1955), and Viktor Frankl (1997) focusing on factors internal to individuals rather than only those externally imposed or environmentally based. Dr Maslow captured this with the term actualization which is a drive of individuals to pursue personal potentials beyond immediate physical needs. And, in his later work (1971), he added the term transcendent actualization which is the desire to reach out beyond the self and contribute to something more than personal needs (discussed in Chapter 5).

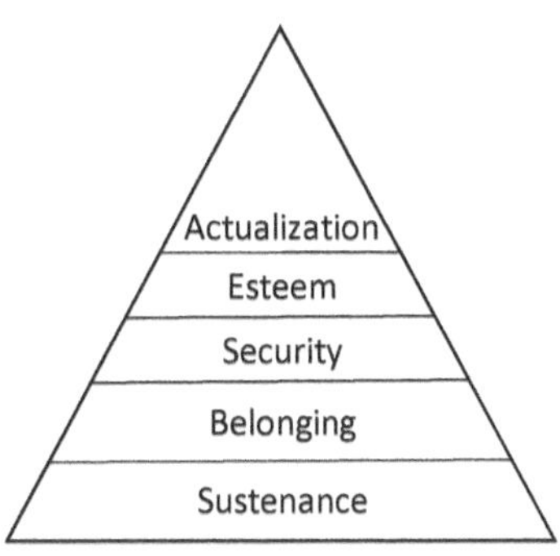


Hierarchy of Needs

This was taken further by Maslow with Theory Z, where individuals pursue potentials external to the self—something bigger or higher than the self. Psychology studies support the importance of the need for an orientation external to the self, and when that involves meaning and explanation of existence, it was called "transcendence" (DeCharms, 1968). This seems to be a fundamental need built into all of us. A major support for this type of transcendence comes from a study of history.

Chapter 5 described how history indicates that ever since people have had the capacity to be conscious of self, they have been concerned about the meaning of their existence, what started and supports it, and existence of something transcendent to the self. Explanations were mysterious and led to religions and many branches of science. Because the answers to these concerns were nebulous and beyond available objective knowledge, people developed metaphysical explanations that became social enterprises with structure and accepted beliefs. Such belief systems formed religions that continue to dominate societies.

Psychological research shows these beliefs are supported by a natural sense of wonderment about the unknown and desire for explanation. This grows out of the ontological imperative discussed in Chapter 3. It results in a fundamental motivation that energizes motives to meet immediate needs, and that supplies meaning and justification for related efforts. It is the drive to find and have meaningful purpose for these efforts, something more than just continuing immediate personal existence, something transcendent to the self.

It should be recognized that the topic here is human motivation. Any form of life has a motivation to exist and to support that existence. It is when a form of life has the capability to be aware of its existence and to process information about it that other motives become important. The more sophisticated and complex a form of life is, the more sophisticated and complex the motives become. For humans, because of a sophisticated consciousness, existence is accompanied by a need for meaning and explanation about that existence. This forms the ontological imperative and the fundamental or basic motivation that energizes motives to meet other needs.

Even though this fundamental motivation seems to be a universal characteristic, it is manifest in many ways. For many people it is not as pressing as those of daily life such as job, food, and entertainment. The less pressing question of why gets pushed into recesses of the subconscious mind where it either creates an unsettled feeling or surfaces unexpectedly. For many people this situation is met by subscribing to answers provided by a belief system already established, one learned in childhood or through subsequent experience. These established systems provide many benefits such as belongingness, social support, moral guidance, salvation, as well as answers to ultimate concerns as explained in Chapter 3.

Dr. Maslow's hierarchy of needs has become popular as a vehicle for improving human health, sense of well-being, and job performance and retention; however, it does not incorporate the needs for meaning, explanation, and purpose proposed by Theory Z and the ultimate need for growth and development that are the essence of actualization. This could be corrected by placing meaning and explanation along with existence and sustenance as an underlying factor for mid-level needs. It would also be helpful to treat the mid-level needs as dimensions rather than hierarchical stages (see Chapter 4). Researchers such as Charlotte Buhler (1967), Anna Freud (1965), and Erik Erikson (1964) showed that any of these needs including meaning and explanation may be pursued at any stage of life. This is illustrated by newborn infants that reach out to explore and learn even when physical needs are met and before they become aware of rewards and punishments (Buhler, 1967).

Need for existence and sustenance accompanied by need for meaning and explanation form the fundamental-level, on which are built the mid-level needs for security, belonging, esteem, and contribution. All of these feed into the top-level need for transcendent actualization which might be summarized as development. A channel should be open for the fundamental needs to bypass the mid-level needs as another dimension, meaning that the mid-level needs do not have to be fulfilled in order for a person to be concerned with the top-level need, although it would help.

<table>
<tr><td colspan="4">Development</td></tr>
<tr><td>Security</td><td>Belonging</td><td>Esteem</td><td>Contribution</td></tr>
<tr><td colspan="4">Explanation</td></tr>
<tr><td colspan="4">Sustenance</td></tr>
</table>

Dimension of Needs

Despite our improved standard of living with its comforts and entertainment, particularly in the United States, there are increasing rates of depression, anxiety, suicide, and criminality. Many people are dissatisfied and have a feeling of meaninglessness or discontent from wanting something more. They are bombarded with media coverage about consumerism, crime, fraud, conflict, and terrorism. Educators cater to radical activists and teach self-enhancement and material wealth. Politicians and community leaders push for power and self-interest. Nations pursue warfare, global conflict, and violence. All of this could be replaced with cooperation and helpfulness if pursuit of the ontological imperative and its resulting needs were emphasized instead and if people thought more about basic motivation—what are we doing that is important and what makes our daily struggles to meet immediate needs worthwhile?

Life was tough for our ancient ancestors and their activities focused on immediate daily needs for survival and sustenance. But they recognized that success and improvement in meeting these daily needs depended on understanding what was going on and for an explanation of the why and what of their existence. They thought a lot about these concerns and developed explanations that contributed to the religions which still dominate cultures and societies. Unfortunately, these religions are losing their benefits now because of conflicts with modern experiences and recent research findings. We need to devote time once again to thinking about these deep questions and recognize our underlying fundamental or basic human motivation. At the core of these deep questions is concern about whether there is an explanation for existence, is there a purpose for it, and if so, what is it, and is this issue important?

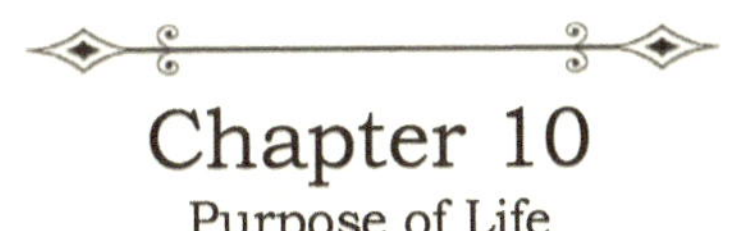

# Chapter 10
### Purpose of Life

We live in a cause-and-effect world. There seems to be cause for things that happen. This opens a way for us to have some influence on our situation and on the things that happen to us. Having cause implies that it has a purpose that produces the effect. Life would, indeed, be chaotic if we did not recognize a purpose for things we experience and have some degree to influence over them. Our ancient ancestors thought a lot about the cause and purpose of their existence because it helped them influence things. Life was tough then and their survival depended on mysterious causes. Assumption and speculation about cause and purpose developed beliefs and religions that continue today to influence culture and civilization. A perennial issue has been the question of whether there really is a cause that gives purpose for our existence. In philosophy the universal attribution of purpose is called teleology and has been a controversial and unresolved topic (McDonough, 2020). So, big questions are: 1) is there a purpose in our existence and for Life in general; if so, 2) what is it; and 3) is it important?

Science has been unable to answer the first question about validity of a purpose for life, but a look at history indicates a probable answer. Chapter 2 gave a brief summary of what is known about the history of our universe and development of life. Studies of history, anthropology, and paleontology show a pattern of continual development in nature toward increasing complexity that enables more effective ways of existing. We modern day humans are the result of this process. There is a pattern of emergent capabilities that shows a design raising the question a designer and purpose. There must have been both, but we do not really know. Whether there was a supernatural Great Creator or a mysterious evolutionary process, is not as important as realizing that this advance of nature exists. Primordial forces combined to form atoms which combined to form molecules which, in turn, combined to form living cells which combined to form animals from which developed humans. Humans with their mental abilities combined to form societies and civilization. The pattern of increasing complexity validates a purpose for our existence. So, here we are, people with sophisticated mental abilities that realize we are part of a changing existence that seems to be pointed to increasing complexity and a continuing process of development.

Science also cannot answer the second question about the nature of life's purpose, but the pattern or thread throughout history indicates the answer is to develop complexity of nature which now involves development of human mental capability and consciousness. This is compatible with the belief built into most religions about a goal of transcending current physical existence for some form of deification that was discussed in Chapter 5. Another approach is the view of a universal type of consciousness of which individual human consciousnesses are aspects thereof (Beichler, 2017). Both develop together as proposed by Panentheism and Process Theology (Simpson, 2013). The "omega point" proposed by Teilhard de Chardin (1965) is the time when we have developed a personal consciousness that melds with the universal consciousness. Eastern ideologies also support this approach with concepts such as reincarnation, Nirvana, and Moksha.

For answer to the third question about importance of this issue, consider the major theme of this book that was presented in Chapter 1 with a brute explanation about the predicted terminal destiny of human life supported by science, philosophy, and religion. The theme is that within one billion years life as we know it will cease—what will happen to human consciousness then?

Chapter 2 presented a summary of the history showing a pattern of continual increase in complexity and sophistication of nature leading to human life that raises the question of whether this pattern of development will continue and produce a form of life that can survive the ultimate global warming. Major changes are now taking place that are similar to major changes that took place during the Axial age and the Enlightenment period. Out of those changes emerged thinking that laid foundations for religions that still dominate societies.

Chapter 3 pointed out that these continuing changes result from a concern about existence and its explanation that is innate to human nature producing the ontological imperative to search for explanation; however, conscious consideration of ultimate concerns has become over-shadowed by concern with immediate daily needs such as wealth, comfort, influence, and entertainment. This submergence of ultimate concerns has decreased the benefits of traditional cultures and religions and stimulated the spirituality movement explained in Chapter 4. Dissatisfaction and difficulties with present-day life have stimulated the search for explanation and the trend toward transcendence explained in Chapter 5.

Chapter 6, then explored the object of these ultimate concerns by considering various views of reality. Reality was further explained in Chapter 7 with information from sub-atomic physics about the basic constituents of our physical world and their relation to our metaphysical world. Outlooks and worldviews that facilitate the pursuit of these concerns were presented in Chapter 8.

Finally, Chapter 9 discussed the role of thinking about ultimate deep concerns and how that energizes motivation to meet more immediate needs. This led to the question about what we are all about and how it related to current personal, domestic, and global problems.

All of this together indicates that to alleviate world problems individuals need to feel that their existence and life in general has design, meaning and purpose. Most religions advocate that the purpose is to do the will of some form of deity, to grow closer to deity, or to join/rejoin deity. The nature of these purposes can only be assumed or revealed by a mystical source because they are beyond scientific investigation.

Many forms of religious beliefs developed with the support of philosophy, literature, and culture. It has already been pointed out that, unfortunately, these beliefs now conflict with research findings and modern experiences to such an extent that traditional beliefs are questioned, and their benefits reduced. There is an urgent need to return to the type of thinking that laid the foundations for religions and cultures. The importance of considering the purpose of life is to rejuvenate thinking about deep concerns, about what is going on.

This book proposes that the most supportable ultimate goal is to foster the continued development in complexity and sophistication of life. Maybe that purpose includes developing a form of life that transcends physical nature and achieves a form of deification. The most complex and sophisticated aspect of life at the present time is human consciousness. Should we not be devoting more effort towards developing human consciousness in addition to explaining its mechanism or ignoring it?

Many secondary goals result. One is to increase our effectiveness so that the daily activities are more efficient and comfortable. This requires additional skill, resources, and knowledge. Another goal is to have relations with and support from fellow humans. There is no animal more dependent on the fellow members of its species than the human (Aronson, 1972). Family, tribe, community, state, and nation are structured to meet this need resulting in many complications that stimulate increased complexity such as individual desires conflicting with community desires, altruism conflicting with self-interest, cooperation competing with competition, and aggression subjugating benevolence.

A third goal grows out of the first two. We have a mental structure that requires sufficient explanation of our existence to make our activities manageable, and meaningful. This has been referred to as worldview, philosophy of life, outlook, etc. It results from the same mental structure that causes realization of the need to grow, to improve, and to wonder about the cause of all of this—why I am here, where did I come from, and where I am going. These are the ultimate concerns introduced in Chapter 3 that result from an innate drive to explain existence and make life more efficient, the ontological imperative. Despite the amazing advance of science, studies of nature have been unable to provide answers to these concerns, so supernatural explanations developed with spiritual and religious beliefs that have dominated societies throughout known history and have been the main impetus for the advance of science, technology, and civilization.

Religion and culture have traditionally ameliorated ultimate concerns by organizing belief systems that not only give answers and explanation, but they also supply resources, support, social structure, and interpersonal relationships. Even the people that do not hold the beliefs of religion and culture live in an environment thusly dominated. These benefits have been quite effective in enabling civilization to advance supplying technologies, comforts, and explanations that have made ultimate concerns less pressing. They have recently become subjugated to more pressing concerns of modern daily existence. The ultimate concerns are eclipsed now by emphasis on consumerism, wealth, competition, politics, and aggression, but they are still there. They lie in the recesses of the subconscious mind creating an unsettling feeling of discontent and may boil up to create emotional turmoil resulting in the current increase in dissatisfaction, depression, anxiety, and suicide. Instead of reaching out for a long-range goal of development, most people mainly pursue short-range goals of meeting immediate desires.

The role of a sense of purpose, feeling of meaning in life, and provision for ultimate concerns are widely recognized as being important for mental health and social issues. Many programs and therapies have been developed to support their benefits for individuals, but problems of discontent continue to increase. Many factors have been proposed for causes of these problems such as: decline in religion due to conflicts between dogma and science; cultural emphasis on consumerism, wealth, and competition; loss of family and community ties; increase in mobility; availability of entertainment and other self-centered activities; and delegation of caregiving and responsibility to government. However, these are all ramifications of the more basic cause of losing sight of the developmental purpose and the need to provide for explanation.

If this innate need for development and answers to ultimate concerns are so important, why are they so neglected? The answer is because we are lazy. We take the easy path. We adopt procedures and explanations that are expeditious for meeting immediate needs. As commercialization developed, supporting these immediate needs became paramount and formed direction for society. Efforts to explain ultimate concerns were replaced with efforts to meet and enjoy immediate needs. Western culture became dominated with "getting and spending," buying and selling material needs. Competition for resources produced conflict, aggression, and violence. Today our major concerns are meeting these material needs. We are bombarded with these goals by TV, radio, newspapers, and magazines. Schools and colleges teach predominantly about these goals with little about ultimate concerns. Leaders and politicians are concerned mainly with their own power and success rather than with ultimate concerns. How different our world would be if media, educators, leaders, and politicians would emphasize the basic need we all have to understand, develop, and grow rather than the current emphasis on consumerism, wealth, self-interest, and power. This would stimulate focus on a higher goal of improving existence.

Many causes have been proposed for the current global and personal problems. And many remedies have also been proposed; however, they all will be ineffective until the emergence of a culture dominated by efforts to move toward something bigger and better than current human concerns. Personal well-being and peace are possible, and despite the current problems, history shows a continuing trend in that direction. Teilhard de Chardin (1965), who was introduced in Chapter 5, supported spiritual evolution as the purpose of existence and a plan of God's that will continue human progress toward the "omega point."

Humans as a species have only about a billion years to pursue this development. The human organism has evolved tremendous abilities during its known history of about 2.5 million years and if nuclear war, overpopulation, or some other mishap does not occur in the next billion years, it could fulfill the positive religious predictions if public society adopts the long-range goal of developing complexity and sophistication of human nature and consciousness so that a form of life emerges that survives material destruction on earth. How does a person's view of this purpose of life relate to their personal well-being, and to their view of the purpose in their own personal life?

# Chapter 11
Purpose in Life

The role of a person's sense of purpose in their personal life (PIL) was introduced at the beginning of this book in the Introduction, and Chapter 3 explained how it was popularized by the famous Austrian psychiatrist Viktor Frankl, who used the term "will to meaning" to emphasize the importance of finding and pursuing a PIL. The essence of this meaning is to find a major goal that supplies a sense of purpose for their life. In his book *Man's Search for Ultimate Meaning*, Frankl (1977) explained the term "noogenic neurosis" as a condition in two-thirds of his psychiatric patients caused by lack of a sense of major purpose. He developed logotherapy to treat this condition.

James Crumbaugh (1973) applied Frankl's concepts in the United States calling his system "logoanalysis," and he developed the Purpose-In-Life test to measure the degree to which an individual had a major goal and was free from the effects of what is called the existential vacuum. This test has stimulated considerable research. The next paragraph summarizes some of this research. You may skip this paragraph if you are not concerned about reliability, validity, and background of this research.

PIL has shown significant negative correlations with confidence (Phillips, 1980), depression and anxiety (Crumbaugh, 1964, Yarnell, 1971). stress coping (Stevens, Pfast & Wessels, 1987); and positive correlations with subjective well-being (Zika & Chamberlain, 1987), time management (Bond & Feather, 1987), defensiveness (Crumbaugh, 1964), and socioeconomic position (Crumbaugh, Raphael, and Shrader, 1970). In studying PIL score differences for various groups of people, Crumbaugh (1964) found a significant difference between "normals" and mental patients, and he found significant differences between ten groups consisting of various socioeconomic and mental health statuses. Successful business and professional personnel and church workers had conspicuously high scores, where alcoholics and neurotics had low scores. Garfield (1973) found significant differences in five subculture groups but pointed out that interpretation of the test items may have contributed to the score differences. Using the Rokeach Value Survey, Crandall and Rasmussen (1975) found that low scores were associated with high value placed on pleasure, comfort, and excitement, while high scores were associated with the value of salvation. Soderstrom and Wright (1977) found high correlation with a religious orientation motivated by an intrinsic personal faith and integrating high moral and spiritual commitment. In a study of male prison inmates, Reker (1979) found a significant correlation with both IQ and age. Reker also found significant correlations with a coherent and favorable self-concept, confidence, orientation toward planning and organizing, and general satisfaction with present life experiences. Three studies conducted at the United States International University found high scores to be related to high sense of meaning in work (Sargent,

1973), low dogmatism and high self-actualization (Ormand, 1973), and low sexual frustration (Sallee and Casciani, 1976). This sampling of research reports shows the usefulness of the PIL concept and value of the Purpose in Life Questionnaire that attempts to measure it.

Other self-report type of measures have been developed to study the role of a person's sense of purpose in their life. The next three paragraphs give information about some of these and can be skipped if you are not interested in the background for my work in this field.

A widely used measure is the Life-Regard Index used to assess two components of a person's sense of purpose: framework which is the conceptualized content and fulfillment that is one's perspective about fulfilling a framework (Battista and Almond, 1973). High life regard scorers were found to have a closer fit with the subcultures and social movements with which the person was involved, and with their ideal self-concept. In studying self-esteem and childhood experiences, a significant difference was found between the high and low scorers. This resulted in the conclusion that development of positive life regard is a two-stage process. First, the individual must develop a positive self-image during late adolescence or early adult life. "The development of a positive life regard, which is the successful resolution of the second stage, is dependent upon the development of self-esteem in the first stage and commitment to fulfillment of life goals" (p. 418).

To measure the individual's feelings about their current position and rate of progress relative to a life goal, Battista and Almond (1973) designed the Life

Orientation Index. The individual first ranks the importance of six major life orientations: interpersonal, service, understanding, obtaining, expressive, and ethical. Then the relative importance of the top three are rated and each is evaluated for its perceived proximity and progress toward attainment. Validity was indicated by significant differences between high and low life regard groups for their most important or their first two most important goals, but not for their third and lower ranked goals. This showed that individuals were able meaningfully to distinguish between life goals options without a generalized halo effect of optimism, pessimism, or similar personality variable. Results also showed that instead of a single encompassing belief, people with positive life regard were often committed to two or more belief systems, suggesting that in our complex society where many religions, values, occupations, and life- styles compete, it may be that purpose in life is derived from an interaction of many sources.

Battista and Almond (1973) pointed out that self-report instruments such as theirs would be prejudiced against persons who have unconscious or non-conceptualized beliefs that serve as a framework for their experiencing of meaning in their lives. Such a subconscious component according to psychoanalysis theory could be expected to conflict with a conscious sense of purpose (SOP) and interfere not only with behavioral consistency, but also on realizing a healthy perception of purpose. This would be similar to libido fixation or personality "hang up." Arnold and Gasson (1954, p. 195) showed that "if there is a gap between the self-ideal as it actually is and the self-ideal as it ought to be, then there will be disturbance." It may be that those low in SOP have been more effectively trained by our current societal influences to subjugate any feeling of purpose that does not produce monetary reward or immediate pleasure. Toler (1974) found that alcoholics and drug addicts place more value on personal goals than societal goals indicating that turning inward away from socially recognized goals may be associated with psychosocial problems. History shows that a greater sense of well-being exists when a person's society is oriented toward long-range idealistic goals and dynamic striving (Campbell, 1975). The passive and hedonistic orientation of our society today could well cause the individual's desire for idealistic efforts and ultimate concerns to be driven into the subconscious mind.

My own experiences in working with people from many different cultures in many different capacities gave me a great interest in the view that people had about their overall sense of purpose in life (SOP) and its relation to their performance and well-being. This interest led me to psychology research. In trying to use Crumbaugh's Purpose-In-Life questionnaire and Battista's Life-Regard-Index to collect data, I found that neither fully captured important aspects of a person's personal view of their purpose in life. So, I developed a questionnaire entitled Life-Esteem-Survey that measured framework (is there a purpose in my life?), perspective (how am I doing in pursuing it?), commitment (how involved am I with it?), and quality (what is the nature of my purpose?).

"Life esteem" I established as the view that people had of their purpose in life. Most researchers that dealt with this topic excluded the nature and content of the framework. Dr. Frankl claimed the nature of one's purpose was not important as long as there was one. My theory was that the view people have of their purpose in life included the quality of the purpose and the degree to which they pursued it or thought it was important for their general well-being—not just feeling good, but also physical, mental, and emotional health. During my work with health promotion, I was able to collect considerable data about life goal orientation and its relationship with health, performance, and well-being.

Reports of many research projects using the Life Esteem Questionnaire are summarized in *Climbing Higher* (Wheeler, 2019). Results of one major project involving 304 public school employees showed that out of twenty-two possible life goals, teachers chose most often belonging (to have companionship, love, and affection). A sample of eighty-six young adults working in various commercial fields chose most often individualization (to find and develop one's own potential). A sample of 205 university students chose understanding (to acquire wisdom and knowledge), and a sample of thirty theology students at the same university chose religion (to live in accordance with belief in a supreme being). These studies confirmed validity, and scores showed a positive relationship of life esteem with general well-being and performance.

Research continues and other methods have been recently developed to measure an individual's view of purpose in life and how it improves in health promotion programs. Major advances have been made in its definition, importance, and enhancement. Martin Seligman, a past president of the American Psychological Association was instrumental in developing "positive psychology" that emphasized health promotion and disease prevention as opposed to disease diagnosis and treatment. In his 2011 book *Flourishing,* Dr. Seligman proposed as the gold standard for measuring well-being the term "flourishing" that consisted of positive emotions, engagement, positive relationships, meaning, purpose, and sense of accomplishment. He reported successful programs aimed at increasing flourishing that reduced post-traumatic stress disorder and medical problems. Although this seems like something new, the term flourishing can be traced back in time to Aristotle who used the ancient Greek term "eudaimonia" to emphasize a goal of effective living in additional to a goal of happiness. This was introduced in Chapter 2. In the book *The Best Within Us*, psychologist Alan Waterman (2013) brought together theory and research information showing the importance of "eudaimonic well-being" that includes flourishing, self-realization, self-concordance (sense of competence), and happiness.

The way people pursue goals varies considerably due to differences in temperament, experiences (learning), and present situation. For example, some people are more goal oriented whereas some are more process oriented. The latter tend to focus on the circumstances of pursuing the goal rather than the final accomplishment. They emphasize the experience and want to "stop to smell the roses" while the more goal-oriented want to push to the intended goal. This applies to life goals also. Some people are more concerned with the pursuit than others are.

This book takes PIL one step further by proposing that an individual's PIL follows from the individual's sense of purpose for life in general (POL) discussed in the previous chapter. If people believe there is a purpose for life and that they are part of life, it follows that they have a purpose. What that is for them personally varies according to their talents, abilities, and attitudes. The famous psychologist Abraham Maslow (1971) popularized this with the term "actualization" which he defined as pursuing personal potential (explained in Chapter 9).

Despite all the research supporting importance for the role of PIL in personal life, there are many people so consumed with daily activities of meeting immediate needs that they have no longer-range goal that gives them an SOP. They usually have a nebulous feeling of dissatisfaction that may emerge with adverse effects. Many people are oblivious to this innate need. Some think there is no need for such a goal and that the consideration is meaningless. Our culture emphasizes goals of meeting immediate daily needs for things like comfort, entertainment, and power. If our culture also emphasized the importance of a POL, people would think more about their own PIL and how that relates to their own well-being. Unsettled feelings of dissatisfaction would be replaced with feelings of accomplishment and contribution. Feelings of worthlessness would be replaced with feelings of valuableness and meaning. An important result of research about PIL is that it follows from the view people have of POL and supplies a valuable meaning in life (MIL), which is recognized as the essence of life satisfaction (Shaver, P & Mikilincer, M, 2012).

# Chapter 12
## Meaning in Life

**P**urpose of life (POL), purpose in life (PIL), sense of purpose (SOP), and meaning in life (MIL) are sometimes used interchangeably when referring to long-range human goals; however, there are subtle differences. POL is a view of a purpose for life in general, reason for the existence of living things. PIL is an objective statement about a major goal in a person's own life. SOP is the subjective personal view of POL and PIL. MIL is a more general term reflecting a view of personal life as being worthwhile and valuable. MIL results from SOP, from seeing a POL and having a PIL. As with sense of purpose, meaning in life has been related to many factors of personal health and well-being, and it has been shown to be a major benefit of religion (Markman, Prouix, & Lindberg, 2013).

Questionnaires have been developed to effectively study the usefulness of MIL. The Meaning in Life Questionnaire measures MIL, PIL, and SOP and has been used in recent research to confirm importance of these concepts (Steger, Frazier, Oishi, & Kaler; 2006). A mass of research and theory about the human need for meaning has been summarized by psychologists Phillip Shaver and Mario Mikilincer (2012) in *Meaning, Mortality, and Choice* supporting meaning as an inherent human need that drives science and social organizations, particularly religion. Examples of topics they relate to in psychology are attachment theory, death anxiety, terror management, and uncertainty tolerance.

Social psychologist Roy Baumeister (1991) who has extensively studied what people want in life concludes that the major desire is to have a meaningful life—it is necessary for happiness. The psychology of meaning has recently advanced from investigation of immediate experiences to investigation of ultimate concerns such as POL and PIL. The architecture of meaning now supports investigation on more than one level (Peterson, 2013). But the sophistication of theories and research reports has clouded resulting information for readers not actively involved in meaning investigation. This topic is of such importance to human well-being that psychology's advances should stimulate involvement for other branches of science and humanities.

The meaning of words allows us to share information and communicate effectively with other people. If we are unsure of a word's meaning, we go to a dictionary (or Google); but where do we go if we are unsure of the meaning of our activities? To feel comfortable in our daily activities and for our efforts to meet every day needs our activities need meaning. They must have reason, purpose, and value. They must fit in with our beliefs, abilities, aspirations, and values. So, whether we are consciously aware of it or not, meaning is important, and it can be considered on several different levels.

An example of the first level occurred this morning when I grabbed a cup of coffee and drove through rush-hour traffic to get to work on time. What was the meaning? It made me a valued employee; it provided a paycheck to support my expenses; it fitted in with my ambitions. That is the first level of meaning, meeting immediate needs and functioning effectively for meeting everyday tasks. This could be called proximate meaning. But for our life to seem valuable, there is more, what could be called distal or secondary meaning.

What is the meaning of getting a paycheck or being a valued employee? Here is an intermediate level. Why fight rush-hour traffic or beat my brains out at that thankless job? What is the meaning of these struggles? There must be more than just getting the paycheck. Many times, we do not think about the reasons for these struggles or their meaning beyond immediate results. We do them because they are there to be done. That is, until something gets upset requiring change in efforts or if questions arise about their value. There must be a deeper meaning to these efforts, a third level that makes them worthwhile beyond immediate or intermediate needs.

Psychologist Paul Wong (2012) who has been an international leader has organized and applied information about meaning emphasizing the importance of meaning-in-life and relating it to spirituality that may explain the third level of meaning. Meaning at this long-range deep level gives people value, fortitude, resilience, purpose, and satisfaction with their existence. It is recognition of something bigger and transcendent to one's personal self and has become associated with spirituality. Spirituality was discussed in Chapter 4 and usually involves faith in a deistic type of power that supplies meaning and purpose for material existence. But belief in God, Yahweh, or Allah with their associated dogma is not required, and maybe all that is needed is belief that there is something beyond the physical view that gives meaning and purpose. This spirituality usually recognizes that ultimate reality may not really be known at the present time.

There usually comes a time when everyone dips down into the deepest level of meaning. What is the meaning of it all? Why am I here; where did I come from; and where am I going? Is there a meaning to my life—is there a purpose for life? These are perennial questions that have been asked as long ago as human history can see. They are the basis of most religions. They are major topics in philosophy and of growing interest in health care fields, particularly psychology. Many fields of science internationally are now contributing objective support to ultimate concerns of meaning in life (Staune, 2006).

We members of the animal species that are called "humans" are in a unique situation. Never before did living beings have immediately available information about happenings world-wide or even universe-wide and find that information useful. If a child is sexually abused in South Africa, we hear about it on the evening news broadcast one minute and the next minute we see pictures of Martian rocks from a newly arrived spacecraft. There is little in our environment about which we do not have information available at our fingertips, eyes, or ears. No longer do we have to wonder what is on the other side of the ocean or why a hurricane destroys a town in Japan. Events that once were only explainable as the result of a mystical supernatural divine force can now be explained as natural processes. But does all of this invalidate the need for mystery, mysticism, and deity? Does it eliminate the meaning, purpose, and support provided by a divine force such as God; and does it release us from the guidance and constraints of a culture based on such beliefs?

Advanced forms of life strive for more than mere survival. They look for patterns and consistencies that enable prediction of events and efficient use of resources (Lent, 2017). Thus, purpose is established, and its pursuit supplies meaning. For humans, though, this search goes even farther. Throughout known history, people have sought explanation for their existence and observed events, and explanation of purpose and meaning that provided for more than just survival. It is not known when this unique human characteristic started, but it seems to have always included a mystical divine force as the cause of things not accounted for. A divine source could be the cause; however, a less esoteric explanation is that human life emerged as neurological complexity increased in the brain—maybe an epiphenomenon of the brain. In any case, the earliest known societies organized beliefs of supernatural force/s as important cause of events. This is the basis of the thousands of religions that have been established, many of which have come and gone (Bowker, 2002).

It is well established that the complexity of human thinking and believing has developed over the passing of time. The earliest known forms of belief attributed animal and human characteristics to supernatural force/s resulting in superstitious forms of animism and shamanism that became more sophisticated with time. In addition to explaining cause of mysterious phenomena, these systems met many needs such as ordering community activities, establishing acceptable behavior, and providing support. Most importantly they supplied a culture of ethics and morals, and a sense of meaning in existence.

Now that we know so much about what is going on, can we use our knowledge to make life more satisfying and the world more comfortable?

Direction for change is emerging from many sources, some of which were mentioned in Chapter 5. The term "flourishing" that was introduced in Chapter 2 and commented on in Chapters 4 and 11 stimulated research in psychology, philosophy, neuroscience, and interdisciplinary studies of history, sociology, anthropology, and medicine. This movement supports a philosophy of life that tolerates differences of opinion and social custom, and supplies a purpose of striving for "eudaimonia," a feeling of satisfaction that one is thriving and that one's actions are contributing to the well-being of oneself and of society (chapter 4). This form of flourishing means having a feeling of meaning for one's own life in the face of adversities and seemingly meaningless situations. It recognizes that there is much beyond our knowledge, that anything is possible, but that we must live in the world as it presents itself to us "here and now," and effectively manage affairs—the pragmatic pluralism world view. And it preserves respect for the mysteries of existence without requiring non-logical explanations while accepting responsibility for personal activities in the process. Many movements are developing to improve MIL but psychology's emphasis on flourishing seems most effective with the potential of breaking enough people away from self-centered striving for material wealth and physical comforts, to cause society to break away from self-interested power struggles that become ends in themselves.

If any of these movements were widely adopted, actions of individuals, organizations, and businesses would be reoriented to reflect a culture based on human well-being and creative development rather than profit, gratification, and entertainment; and nations would reduce global conflicts. Public media could then foster deeper thinking and a beneficial sense of ultimate meaning. Our culture would emphasize the purpose of life and the importance of pursuing a personal purpose in life oriented toward growing greater complexity and sophistication and contributing to that growth for other people and for the human species. Progress will then be made toward developing some form of life or consciousness that survives the predicted destruction of physical existence as we know it. The ultimate goal is beyond our present-day grasp, but if enough people thought about these ultimate concerns, world problems would be reduced, and well-being would be increased. Despite the long-range idealistic nature of this goal, the mere process of being concerned with and pursuing it would produce benefits if the process was brought out of hiding and emphasized.

# Epilogue

Even though this book proposes an answer to the question about the purpose of life, that answer involves consideration of long-rang idealistic tasks and more deep questions. Advancing through the nonagenarian years and losing many contemporary friends and relatives causes me to look back on my years and wonder what it is all really about. I have always tried to balance improving myself for the future with meeting immediate needs and desires. There were times when tasks were so difficult that I did not know how I was going to succeed. There were times of anguish over hardships and failures. Then there were times of elation over successes and accomplishments, and times of inspiration over glimpses of insight and progress. Most importantly, though, there have been times of confusion and doubt over why all of this was happening—did it have meaning and purpose? Some people seem secure in religious beliefs that answer that question, but conflicts between dogmatic beliefs and objective knowledge have made these beliefs questionable for me. Now, though, I feel a sense of contentment and satisfaction that it all fits together as part of an evolving scheme moving towards something bigger and better than my personal self and those around me—toward some type of existence transcendent to our observable environment.

*Survival of Life*

A major source of wonder has been the question of whether my situation is the result of creation by a transcendent deity that may still provide influence or the result of adaptive evolution, and whether my mind is only an epiphenomenon of my brain's neurological processes or if it has an existence independent of my body. It amazes me to realize that these questions have now lost their importance. It does not seem to make much difference whether there really is a deity or not, because what is now known about our environment and its history indicates that it could be either way, or even both ways at the same time—a great paradox from need to both believe and doubt.

Recent scientific findings show that despite the extensive knowledge available about our universe, our view is limited and there is much beyond our view that may extend to an eternity within which anything and everything exists, even other universes and God. However, an esoteric metaphysical power is not necessary to explain this existence, and the boundary between physical and metaphysical or between natural and supernatural is now obscure.

History and anthropology show that ever since humans were capable of abstract reasoning, they have been dominated by belief systems involving transcendent powerful deities. These beliefs have been instrumental in advancing civilization, culture, welfare, and the comforts we now enjoy. They have produced challenges and tensions without which development and technology would have languished.

Psychology, sociology, and physiology show that religious beliefs and religions have alleviated many human needs including support, belongingness, forgiveness, charity, fraternity, coherence, certainty, meaning, and purpose. However, conflicts with modern experiences and research findings are causing many people to abandon traditional religions losing these benefits. The recent increase in personal dissatisfaction, anxiety, depression; community murder, robbery, violence; and global aggression, terrorism, conflict have been attributed to this loss. Our distant ancestors thought a lot about meaning of life and developed these religions that still dominate society. We need to resume such thinking and update religions.

I do not know if God or any other esoteric power really exists and I do not rely on favors from such power, but as I try to draw conclusions from my experiences and accumulated knowledge a sense of respect and wonder about the unknown creates in me a feeling of awe and reverence. So, what does all this mean? What is its impact? I am content with the realization that I (and we) do not know and that the answers may be unknowable, and that I can enjoy pursuing an ontological quest with a feeling of development, unfolding, contribution, and flourishing. Soon I will take the biggest step in that pursuit—the ultimate experience in the quest for knowledge about whether there is really anything beyond mortal existence. And when it is all over...

"... When my work is done,
My course on earth is run,
May it be said, well done,
Be thou at peace."

(West Point Alma mater, Reinecke)

# Glossary

*Some important terms use selected definitions, and some new terms are introduced.*

**Consciousness** – 1) Awareness of the environment which all living things have to some degree. For sophisticated humans this includes being aware of oneself and thought processes. 2) A component in all of nature that gives everything vitality. 3) A fundamental constituent of nature.

**Dualism** – Philosophical approach to explaining nature as consisting of both mental and physical constituents.

**Eschaton** – End of current human life predicted by many religions.

**Eudaimonia** – Ancient Greek term that has come to represent a high state of well-being and satisfaction with life.

**Flourishing** – A modern term similar to eudaimonia that represents a high state of well-being from participating in satisfying activities.

**FC - Fundamental Constituent** – The most fundamental thing that underlies the parts of nature. Sub-atomic physicists have supported through indirect observations things such as fields or forces that might be the result of such things as information, consciousness, or spirit.

**Idealism** – The philosophical approach to explaining nature as being the result of consciousness or some type of mental activity.

**Life Esteem** – A person's view of the value, purpose, and meaning of life.

**Materialism** – The philosophical approach to explaining nature as being the result of developing physical material. It is similar to physicalism that sees all things (even mental) as having a material base.

**Metaphysical** – Beyond physical nature.

**MIL** - **Meaning in Life**. A person's view of their life as having value and purpose.

**Nature** – The physical environment

**Ontos** – Ancient Greek term for ultimate being, underlying cause of existence.

**Ontological Engineering** – Attempts to apply the ontological imperative for human benefit.

**Ontological Imperative** – Need built into all humans to search for explanation of existence, the what, why, how, and source of life.

**Ontological Research** – Research and study resulting from the ontological imperative.

**PIL** – **Purpose in life**. A person's view of a long-range goal or major purpose in their life.

**POL** – **Purpose of life** in general.

**Pluralism** – Philosophical approach to explaining nature as consisting of multiple possible alternate realities in addition to our own.

**Panpsychism** – Philosophical approach to explaining nature as being the result of consciousness, all things have a degree of consciousness.

**Panprotopsychism** – Philosophical approach to explaining nature as the result of something more basic than consciousness that could be called protoconsciousness. Not everything is conscious, but everything has consciousness and protoconsciousness in the parts that make it up.

**Physicalism** – Philosophical approach to explaining nature as being physical, even mental things are physically based.

**Pragmatic Pluralism** - Proposed worldview or philosophy that recognizes the possibility of alternate realities and that although anything is possible, however we must live in the world as it presents itself to us in the "here and now."

**Reality** – The basic aspect of existence that is consistent, true, and actual.

**Reality, Existential** – View of reality based on recognizing problems of existence and accepting responsibly for their management.

**Reality, Personal** – Personal overall subjective view of reality.

**Reality, Pragmatic** – View of reality based on usefulness as opposed to truth.

**Reality, Universal** – View of reality as being fixed, unchanging, and universal.

**Religion** – An organized belief about a divine or transcendent power that is shared with others usually in a structured setting.

**SOP** – **Sense of purpose**. A person's view that their life has a long-range goal or major purpose.

**Spirituality** - An attitude of concern about a realm above and beyond oneself.

**Supernatural** – Beyond physical nature. Similar to metaphysical.

**Theism** - Philosophical approach to explaining nature as being the result of a Divine power.

**Transcendence** - Process of moving into a realm beyond immediate existence.

**Ultimate Concerns** – Concerns about deep things of
life such as source, purpose, and the whys and
wherefores of existence.

# References

Abrams, S. (2015). *A God that could be real.* Boston: Beacon Press.

Allport, G.W. (1955). *Becoming.* New York: Yale University Press.

Amoroso, R. & Martin, B. (2002). Consciousness: a thousand points of life. *Noetic Journal. 3 (4),* 289.

Armstrong, K. (2000). *The battle for God.* New York: Knopf.

Arnold, M. & Gasson, J. (1954). *The human person.* New York: Ronald Press.

Aronson, E. (1972). *The social animal.* San Francisco: Freeman.

Attridge, H. (2009). *The religion and science debate.* New Haven: Yale University Press.

Batson, D; Schoenrade, P.; & Ventis, W. (1993). *The religious and the individual: a social-psychological perspective.* New York: Oxford.

Battista, J. & Almond, R. (1973). The development of meaning in life. *Psychiatry, 36,* 409.

Baumeiater, R. (1991). *Meanings of life.* New York: Guilford.

Baumiester, R. (2005). *The Cultural Animal.* New York: Oxford University Press.

Beichler, J. (2017). Consciousness manifesto: physical origins of consciousness through evolution and revolution. *WISE Journal.*

Bible (1976). King James version. Nashville, TN: Thomas Nelson.

Braisby, N. (1012). *Cognitive psychology*. NY: Oxford University Press USA.

Buhler, C. (1967). Human life goals in the humanistic perspective. *Journal of Humanistic Psychology. 7*, 36.

Calaprice, A. (2005). *The new quotable Einstein.* Princeton, NJ: Princeton University Press.

Campbell, C. (1975, February). Coming apart at the seams (interview with Robert Heilbroner). *Psychology Today*, 95-103.

Chalmers, D. (2022). Reality+. New York: Norton.4

Clayton, P. & Knapp, S. (2011). *The predicament of belief.* New York: Oxford.

Cloninger, R. (2004). *Feeling good.* New York: Oxford.

Comstock, G. & Partridge, K. (1972). Church attendence and health. *Journal of Chronic Disease, 25 (12)*, 665-672.

Crandall, J. & Rasmussen, R. (1975). PIL as related to specific values. *Journal of Clinical Psychology, 31(3)*, 483.

Crumbaugh, J. (1973). *Everything to gain.* Chicago: Nelson-Hall.

Crumbaugh, J. & Maholick, L. (1964). An experimental study in existentialism: the psychometric approach to Frankl's concept of noogenic neurosis. *Journal of Clinical Psychology, 20(2)*, 200-207.

Crumbaugh, J., Raphael, M. & Shrader, R. (1970). Frankl's will to meaning in a religious order. *Journal of Clinical Psychology, 26(2)*, 206-207.

Davies, P. (2008). *The goldilocks enigma.* New York: Houghton Mifflin.

DeCharmes, R. (1968). *Personal causation.* New York; Academic Press.

DiBiase, F. (2009). A holographic model of consciousness. *Quantum Biosystems. 3,* 207-220.

Ellis, G. (2011). Does the universe really exist? *Scientific American.* August, 38-53.

Ellison, C. W. (1983). Toward an integrative measure of health and well-being. *Journal of Psychology and Theology, 19,* 35-48.

Emmons, R. (1999). *The psychology of ultimate concerns.* New York: Guilford.

Erikson, E. (1964). *Insight and Responsibility.* New York: Norton.

Flanagan, O. (2009). *The really hard problem.* Cambridge, MA: MIT Press.

Fowler, J. (1981). *Stages of faith.* San Francisco: Harper.

Frankl, V.E. (1997). *Man's search for ultimate meaning.* New York: Plenum Press.

Freud, A. (1965). Normality and pathology in childhood: Assessments of development. In *Writings (Vol.6).* New York: International Universities Press.

Fromm, E. (1947). *Man for himself.* Greenwich, CT: Fawcett.

Garfield, C. (1973). A psychometric and clinical investigation of Frankl's concept of existential vacuum and of anomia. *Psychiatry, 36,* 396-408.

Goff, P. (2019). *Galileo's error: foundations for a new science of consciousness.* NY: Pantheon.

Goff, P., Seager, W., Allen-Hermanson, S. (2022). Panpsychism. *The Stanford Encyclopedia of Philosophy.* https://plato.stanford.edu/entries/panpsychism.

Goodenough, U. (1998). *The sacred depths of nature.* New York: Oxford.

Hamer, D. (2004). *The God gene.* New York: Doubleday.

Haisch, B. (2010). *The purpose guided universe.* Franklin Lakes, NJ: Career Press.

Hardy, C. (2016). ISS theory: cosmic consciousness, self, &life beyond death in a hyperdimensional physics. *Journal of Consciousness Exploration & Research. 7 (11),* 1012-1035.

Hausoul, R. (2019). Theology and cosmology: call for interdisciplinary enrichment. *Zygon, 54(2),* 324-336.

Heckel, E. (1992). *The riddle of the universe.* Buffalo, NY: Prometeous.

Heid, M. (2021). Why human beings are hardwired for spirituality and magical thinking. *http://elemental.meduim.com,* 3/12/2021.

Heider, F. (1944). Social perception and phenomenal causality. *Psychological Review, 51,* 358-374.

Heintzelman, S. & King, L. (2014). Life is meaningful. *American Psychologist,* 69(6), 561-574.

Helmenstine, A. (2021). Seven extinction level events that could end life as we know it. *ThoughtCo. http://www.thoughtco.com/extinction-level-events-4158931,* 2/17/2021.

Hooker, S. A., Masters, K. S., & Park, C. L. (2017, July 6). A meaningful life is healthy life. *Review of General Psychology.* Advance online publication. dx.doi.org/10.1037/gpr0000115

Huxley, A. (1944). *The perennial philosophical.* New York: Harper & Row.

James, W. (2006). *A pluralistic universe.* Charleston, SC: Bibliobazaar.

Jeans, J. (1933). *The new background of science.* New York: Macmillion.

Jeeves, M. & Brown, W. (2009). *Neuroscience, Psychology and Religion.* Conshohocken, PA: Templeton Foundation Press.

Jung, C.G. (1938). *Psychology and religion.* London: Yale University Press

Kaufman, G. (2006). *Jesus and creativity.* Minneapolis: Fortress Press.

Kaufman, S. (2020). *Transcendence.* New York: TarcherPerigee.

Kauffman, S. (2008). *Reinventing the sacred.* New York: Basic Books.

Kohlberg, L. (1984). *The psychology of moral development: the nature and validity of moral stages.* New York: Addison Wesley.

Kuhlmann, M. (3013). What is real? *Scientific American,* 41-17.

Kurtz, P. (2007). *What is secular humanism?* Amherst, NY: Prometheus Books.

Lent, J. (2017). The patterning instinct. New York: Prometheus Books.

Lincoln, D. (2012). The universe is a complex & intricate place. *Scientific American.* 38-43.

Lohrey, A. (2018) *The evolution of consciousness.* Princeton, NJ: ICRL Press.

Kohlberg, L. (1984). *The psychology of moral development.* New York: Addison Wesley

Mackey, A. (1921). *An encyclopedia of Freemasonry.* New York: Masonic History Company.

Markman, K., Prouix, T., & Lindberg, M. (Ed). (2013). *The psychology of meaning.* Washington DC: American Psychological Association.

Maslow, A. (1968). *Toward a psychology of being.* (2nd Ed.). New York: Harper & Row.

Maslow, A. (1971). *The farther reaches of human nature.* New York: Viking.

May, R. (1967). *Psychology and the human dilemma.* New York: Norton.

McCall, B. (2010). Kenosis and emergence: a theological synthesis. *Zygon, 45(1),*149-164.

McDonough, J. (Ed.) (2020). Teleology: a history. New York: Oxford University.

McGregor, D. (2006). *The human side of enterprise, annotated edition.* New York: Mcgraw-Hill.

Nelson, J. (2009). *Psychology, religion, and spirituality.* New York: Springer.

Newberg, A. (2010). *Principle of neurotheology.* Burlington, VT: Ashgate.

Newberg, A. & D'Aquili, E. (2001). *Why God won't go away.* New York: Ballantine Books.

Newman, D., Schneider, S., & Stone, A. (2022). Contrasting effects of finding meaning and searching for meaning, and political orientation and religiosity, on feelings and behaviors during the COVID-19 pandemic. *Personality & Social Psychology Bulletin. 48(6),* 923-936.

Ormand, H. (1973). Relationship of measurements of dogmatism, PIL and self-actualization. *Dissertation Abstracts, 34(48),* 1730.

Paloutzian, R. & Park, C. (Eds.) (2005). *Handbook of the psychology of religion and psychology.* New York: Guilford.

Pearce, J. (2002). *The biology of transcendence.* Rochester, VT: Park Street Press.

PewForum (2019). *Pew Research Center. www.pewforum.com,* 10/17/2019.

Pfeiffer, J. (1969). *The emergence of man.* New York: Harper & Row.

Phillips, W. (1980). Purpose in life, depression, and locus of control. *Journal of Clinical Psychology, 36(3),* 661-667.

Pihlstrom, S. (2013). *Pragmatic pluralism & the problem of God.* NY: Fordham University Press.

Polkinghorne, J. (2007). Science and religion: Bottom-up style, interface context. *Zygon, 42(3),* 573-576.

Powell, D. (2018). The standard model. *Discover, JulyAugust,*68-69.

Radin, D. (2013). *Supernormal.* New York: Deepak Chopra Books.

Reker, G. & Cousins, J. (1979). Factor structure construct validity and reliability of the Seeking of Noetic Goals (SONG) and Purpose in Life (PIL) tests. *Journal of Clinical Psychology, 35(1),* 85-91.

Rican, P. & Janosova, P. (2010). Spirituality as a basic aspect of personality: A cross-cultural verification of Piedmont's model. *International Journal for the Psychology of Religion, 20,* 2.

Robinson, D. (2020). Idealism. *Encyclopedia Britannia,* Britannia. Com.

Rogers, C. (1961). *On becoming a person.* Boston: Houghton Mifflin.

Russell, B. (2009). *An outline of philosophy.* Omon: Routledge.

Sargent, G. (1973). Motivation and meaning: Frankl's logotherapy in the work situation. *Dissertation Abstracts, 34(48),* 1785.

Selligman, M. (2011). *Flourish.* New York: Free Press.

Severin, F. (1973). *Discovering man in psychology.* New York: McGraw-Hill.

Service, R. (2015). Researchers may have solved the end-of-life conundrum. *Science Magazine, https://www.sciencemag.org/news/2015/03/*

Shah, K. (2021). Most life on earth will be killed by lack of oxygen in a billion years. *New Scientists, https://www.newscientist.com*, 3/1/2021.

Shaver, P. & Mikulincer, M. (Eds) (2012). *Meaning, morality, and choice.* Washington DC: American Psychological Association.

Simpson, Z. (2013). Emergence and non-personal theology. *Zygon, 48(2),*405-426.

Soderstrom, D. & Wright, E. (1977). Religious orientation and meaning in life. *Journal of Clinical Psychology, 33(1),* 65-68.

Smith, E. (2017). *The power of meaning.* New York: Crown.

Spilka, B; Hood, R.; Hunsberger, B.; & Garsuch, R. (2003). *The psychology of religion* (3d Ed.). New York: Guilford.

Stephen, C. (2021). Here are 5 fascinating types of universes. http://www.medium.com, 3/12/2021

Steger, M., Frazier, P., Oishi, S., & Kaler, M. (2006). The Meaning in Life Questionnaire: Assessing the presence of and search for meaning in life. *Journal of Counseling Psychology, 53,* 80-93.

Stevens, M., Pfost., K. & Wessels, A. (1987). The relationship of purpose in life to coping strategies and time since death of a significant other. *Journal of Counseling & Development, 65(8),* 424-426.

Szocik, K. (2017). Religion and religious beliefs as evolutionary adaptions. *Zygon,* 53(1), 24-51.

Teilhard de Chardin, P. (1965). *The phenomenon of man.* (B. Wall, Trans.). New York: Harper & Row.

Toler, C. (1974). The personal values of alcoholics and addicts. *Newsletter for Research in Mental Health & Behavioral Sciences, 16(3),* 17.

Tirosh-Samuelson, H. (2012). Transhumanism as a secular faith. *Zygon, 47(4),*710-734.

Vaillant, G. E. (2008). *Spiritual development.* New York: Broadway Books.

Walker, E. (2000). *The physics of consciousness.* Cambridge, MA: Perseus Books.

Weissenbacher, A. (2018). Moral enhancement and deification through technology. *Theology and Science,* 16(3),243-246.

Wheeler, J. A. (1997*). At home in the universe.* NY: American Institute of Physics.

Wheeler, R.; Munz, D.; & Jain, A. (1990). Life goals and general well-being. *Psychological Reports, 66,* 307-312.

Wheeler, R. (2010). *Mountains and Minds.* Bloomington, IN: Xlibris.

Wheeler, R. (2019). *Climbing higher: answering big questions.* St Louis: OntoScience Press.

Wheeler, R. (2021). *What, why, and how?* St Louis: OntosScience Press.

Wong, P. & Fry, P. (1998). *The human quest for meaning.* Mahwah, NJ: Erlbaum.

Yarnell, T. (1971). PIL test: further correlates. *Journal of Individual Psychology, 27,* 76.

Zika, S. & Chamberlain, K. (1987). Relation of hassles and personality to subjective well-being. *Journal of Personality & Social Psychology, 53(1),* 155-162.

# Author

obert Wheeler developed a keen interest in the view people have about meaning and purpose in their lives during 20 years of military experience working with people of various cultures as an infantryman, aviator, engineer, advisor, and research & development coordinator. His last assignment before retiring was Chief of the Foreign Technology Office at the U.S. Army Aviation Systems Command. For another 20 years, he filled positions at St Louis University to include Director of Health Promotion Research and adjunct Associate Professor of Psychology. His major work was research about personality characteristics that contribute to health, well-being, and performance. He also developed measuring instruments and performed analyses for health promotion programs from a didactic viewpoint to assist participants, from an evaluation viewpoint to determine effectiveness, and from a research viewpoint to increase knowledge of health enhancement and quality of life improvement. Now retired, his current work is with spirituality as a personality characteristic, and its role in human nature and health. He also remains physically active. In 2014 he set a new Guinness World Book Record as the oldest man to climb Mount Kilimanjaro in Africa.

# Other books by Robert Wheeler

*Mountains and Minds.* (2010). Bloomington, IN: Xlibris.
*Climbing Higher.* (2019). St Louis: OntosScience.
*What, Why, and How?* (2021). St Louis: OntosScience.

# Website

### www.ontossciene.com

**Ontos** is an ancient Greek word meaning fundamental being, ultimate reality, or meaning of existence. **OntosScience** attempts to explore this in a sensible way consistent with experience and science.

The goal of **OntosScience** is to make people more aware of the **"ontological imperative."** This is our innate need to strive for a sense of purpose that gives meaning to our lives. That striving has been related to personal health, well-being, and performance.

The homepage menu has links to **Blog & Comment**, **contact webmaster**, **publication summaries & reviews**, and selected **short articles** about important life questions.

Please post a comment.

# Index

A

Abraham Maslow 17, 33, 42, 90
Activists 20, 71
Actualization 28, 34, 43, 66–67, 69–70, 90
Actualizers 35, 43
Actualizing 35
Adaptability 7
Addicts 87
Adolescence 85
Adversities 11, 96
Aether 54
Africa 4, 10, 94
Aggression 12–13, 16, 77–79, 101
Aggressive 12, 65
Agnosticism 63
Alan Waterman 89
Albert Einstein 35, 61
Albert Mackey 32
Alcoholics 84, 87
Aldous 24
Aldous Huxley 24
Allegories 32
Allen-Hermanson 53
Almond 85–86
Altruism 77
American 12, 88
Amoroso 55

Ancestors 8, 38, 71, 73, 101
Andrew Newberg 24
Animism 5, 95
Anna Freud 34, 69
Anthropologists 4
Anthropology 4, 11, 59, 74, 96, 100
Anthropomorphic 46
Anxiety 8, 13, 16, 20, 33, 40, 43, 64–65, 71, 78, 83, 92, 101
Apologists 31
Archeologists 4
Aristotle 89
Armstrong 6
Arnold 86
Aronson 77
Artificial Intelligence 40
Astronomers 23
Astrophysicist 30, 60
Atheism 26, 63
Atheistic 10
Atman 56
Atom 23, 49, 51, 60
Atoms 2–3, 6, 51, 60, 74
Australia 4
Axial Age 6, 9, 75

# B

Batson 29
Battista 85–86
Battista's 87
Baumeister 4, 92
Believers 10, 12

Belongingness 18, 66, 69, 100
Bernard 60
Bertrand Russell 53
Bible 32, 39, 55
Big Bang 2
Big Questions 11, 47, 73
Biochemist Stuart Kauffman 25
Brain 3–4, 7, 24, 29–30, 55, 95
British 53
Buddha 5, 46

# C

Calaprice 35
Campbell 87
Carl Rogers 24
Casciani 85
Cause-and-Effect 73
Chamberlain 84
Chardin 41, 75, 80
Charlotte Buhler 69
China 4
Christian 5, 31, 41
Christian Dogma 5
Christianity 2, 5–6, 25
Church 14–16, 21, 25, 84
Civilization 4, 6, 12, 45, 47, 59, 65–66, 73–74, 78, 100
Civilizations 4
Climate Change 1, 9
Climbing Higher 47, 88
Coalescence 52
Cognitive 4–5, 24, 35
Cognitive Ability 4–5, 35

Cognitive Process 24

Coherence 59, 100

Commercialization 79

Conceptualization 36

Confucius 5

Consciousness 2–3, 7, 13, 41–42, 49, 51–56, 60, 68, 74–75, 77,
81, 97, 103–105

Consumerism 20, 66, 71, 78–80

Contemporary 48, 53, 99

Cosmic 52–53, 56

Cosmic-Consciousness 59

Cosmology 1

Crandall and Rasmussen 84

Creative Abilities 33

Creative Design 2

Creative Development 97

Creative Force 46

Creative Process 46

Creativity 12, 15, 31, 35, 54

Creator 6, 18, 30–31, 42, 74

Crime 8, 20, 40, 43, 45, 65, 71

Criminality 20, 71

Crisis 9

Crumbaugh, Raphael, and Shrader 84

Cultural 24, 29, 79

Culture 4–7, 9–10, 12, 14, 17, 31, 43, 45–46, 73, 76, 78–80, 90,
95–97, 100

Cyclic-Universe 59

# D

David Chalmers 48

Davies 61

Dean 24

Dean Hamer 24

Debiase 55

Decharms 67

Deep Questions 24, 45, 71, 99

Deep Thinking 44

Defensiveness 84

Deficiency Needs 33–34, 36

Definition: "…Transcendence of 43

Definition of Pragmatic 63

Definition of Transcendence 43

Deities 30, 61, 100

Deity 10, 18, 23, 28, 30, 35, 52, 63, 76, 94, 100

Depression 8, 13, 16, 20, 40, 43, 64–65, 70, 78, 83, 101

Determinism 17

Dimension 34–37, 70

Dimensions 33–37, 69

Disease 11, 89

Disease Diagnosis 89

Disease Prevention 89

Divine Force 19, 35, 94–95

Divine Knowledge 28

Divine Power 45–46, 105

Divine Realm 12, 28

Divinity 31–32

Dogma 5–6, 14–15, 25–26, 30–32, 36, 63, 79, 94

Dogmatism 85

Douglas McGregor 66

Drug Addicts 87

Dualism 53–54, 62, 103

# E

Earth 1–2, 39, 41, 43, 81, 101
Earthly Existence 39, 41
Eastern 75
Eastern Ideologies 75
Ecclesiastical Dogma 31
Economic 9, 16
Education 9
Educators 20, 66, 71, 80
Ego 43–44
Egocentric 34
Egypt 4
Eighteenth Century 15
Eighteenth-Century 6
Ellis 23
Ellison 26
Emergence 2–3, 13, 28, 30–31, 80
Emotional Health 88
Emotional Turmoil 78
Employees 66, 88
Encyclopedia of Freemasonry 32
Enoch 39
Entangled 60
Epilogue 99
Epiphenomenon 95, 100
Epistemology 48
Erich Fromm 33
Erik Erikson 69
Eschatology 1
Eschaton 41, 103

Esoteric Self-Transcendence 24

Esteem 67, 70, 87–88, 104

Ethe 99

Ethical Society 14, 25

Ethics 5, 59, 63, 96

Eudaimonia 11, 89, 96, 103

Europe 15

Evan Walker 60

Evolution 2, 19, 29, 59, 80, 100

Evolutionary Process 6, 74

Evolve 2, 41

Existence 1, 3–5, 8, 10–11, 13, 15–18, 20–21, 23–24, 27–28, 31, 33, 37–41, 43–45, 48, 54, 59, 62, 64, 67–71, 73–78, 80, 91, 93, 95–97, 99–101, 104–106

Existential 17, 33, 47, 83, 105

Existential Reality 47

Existential Vacuum 83

Extraterrestrial Beings 23


# F

Fear 9, 43, 63

Feather 84

Fermions 54, 56, 61

Flanagan 11, 28

Flourishing 11, 28, 89, 96, 101, 103

Fourth Dimension 35

Freemasonry 31–32

French 41

Fundamentalist 10


# G

Galileo's Error 53
Gallop  Poll 14
Garfield 84
Gasson 86
Genesis 55
George Vaillant 29
God 14, 18, 20, 23, 30–32, 39, 41–43, 45–46, 48, 52, 55–56, 60,
    63, 93, 95, 100–101
God's Will 28
Goodenough 25
Gordon Allport 17, 67
Gordon Kaufman 31
Gorsuch 26
Great Architect 19, 32, 46, 60
Great Creator 6, 74
Greek 5, 18, 41, 54, 60, 89, 103–104
Greek Philosopher 41
Greek Philosophy 5
Greek Word 18, 54, 60

# H

Haisch 52, 60
Happiness 89, 92
Hardy 55
Hausoul 2
Heaven 39, 42
Hebrews 39
Heid 30
Heider 23
Helmenstine 1
Homocentric 35
Hood 26

Hooker 19

Human 1–5, 7, 9–10, 13, 18–20, 25, 27–30, 32–33, 38, 40–43, 46–47, 53, 59, 62–63, 65–66, 68–69, 71, 74–75, 77, 80, 91–92, 94–95, 97, 100, 103–104

Humanism 5

Humanistic 17, 19, 42, 66–67

Hunsberger 26

Hyper-Dimension 51


# I

Idealism 52–53, 103

Ideation 36

Ideological Aggression 16

Immortality 59

Individualization 88

Inequality 10

Infinite 23

Infinity 61

Injustice 10

Intelligence 2, 7, 13, 27, 35, 40, 48–49, 51, 60–61

Intelligent-Design 59

Iraq 4

Irenaeus 41

Islam 6, 25


# J

James Crumbaugh 83

James Fowler 36

Jane Loevenger's 44

Jannah 42

Janosova 27

Japan 94
Jeeves 3
Jesuit 41
Jesus 31, 46
Job 18, 46, 66, 69, 93
Joel Primack 30
John 32, 41, 55
John Polkinghorne 41
John Wheeler 55
Judaism 5, 25

# K

Kaler 91
Kevin Nelson 24
King Solomon 31
Kuhlmann 51, 55, 61

# L

Laozi 5
Lawrence Kohlberg 36
Laws of Nature 61
Leptons 55, 61
Libido 86
Life-Esteem-Survey 87
Life-Regard 85
Life-Regard-Index 87
Life-Space 24
Lifespan 65
Light 30, 55
Lincoln 55

Lindberg 91
Literature 76
Logoanalysis 83
Logotherapy 83
Lohrey 53

# M

 Macrocosm 23, 61
Many-Worlds 59
Man's Search For Ultimate 83
Mario Mikilincer 91
Markman 91
Martian 94
Martin 55, 88
Master Spirit 46
Materialism 17, 51, 53, 104
Materialistic 51–52, 57
Matter 2, 7, 13, 19, 42, 48, 51–52, 55–56, 60–61
Matter-Energy 60
Mccall 2
Mcdonough 73
Meaning, Mortality, and Choice 91
Media 16, 20, 66, 71, 80, 97
Merriam-Webster 40, 45
Mesopotamia 4
Metaneeds 33–34, 36, 66
Meta-Needs 43
Metaphysical 40, 46, 55, 62, 68, 76, 100, 104–105
Metaphysics 56
Microcosm 23, 60–61
Middle East 10
Mil 19, 90–91, 96, 104

Militant Atheism 26
Mind 3, 18, 30, 34–35, 40, 56, 60, 69, 78, 87, 100
Mohammad 46
Moksha 75
Molecules 3–4, 6, 74
Multiverse 51, 59
Mystical Phenomena 59
Mystical Realm 24, 38
Mystical Transcendent Realm 25
Mysticism 25–26, 94

# N

Nancy Adams 30
Natural Evolution 2
Naturalism 14, 25, 56
Natural Phenomena 25
Natural Processes 94
Natural Resources 13
Neurobiologist 24
Neurological 25, 95, 100
Neuroscience 3, 11, 28, 59, 96
Neurosis 83
Neurotheology 25
Neurotics 84
Newman, Schneider, & Stone 29
Nirvana 42, 75
Noetic Fields 55
Nonagenarian 99
Nonbelievers 12
Non-Believers 7
Nonmaterial 7
Non-Material 25, 42

Non-Material-Like 54
Nonphysical 2
Nontranscendent 35
Noogenic Neurosis 83

## O

Object 18, 20, 32, 37, 45–46, 60, 76
Objective Explanation 19
Objective Knowledge 47, 68, 99
Objective Statement 91
Objective Support 94
Objective Thinking 6
Observable Environment 44, 99
Observable Nature 18
Observable Physical 35
Oishi 91
Omega Point 41, 75, 80
Ontological 16–21, 27, 34–35, 37, 40, 44–45, 57, 59, 64, 68–
    69, 71, 75, 78, 101, 104
Ontology 18, 20
Ontos 18, 20, 54, 104
Ontoscentric 34
Ontosscience 20
Organism 41, 80
Otherworldliness 38
Owen Flanagan 28

## P

Paleontologist 41
Paleontology 2, 6, 74
Paloutzian 26

Paloutzian & Park 26

Panentheism 30, 75

Panpsychicism 53

Panpsychism 53, 104

Paradox 56, 100

Park 19, 26

Pathology 11

Paul Wong 93

Pearce 40

Perception 54, 86

Perennial Philosophy 24

Perennial Questions 45, 94

Permanent 45

Pessimism 86

Peterson 92

Pew Research Center 14

Pfeiffer 4

Phenomena 5, 25, 27, 49, 52, 54, 59, 95

Philip Clayton 30

Philip Goff 53

Phillips 83

Phillip Shaver 91

Philosopher 28, 41, 48, 53, 63

Philosophers 63

Philosophical Approach 103–105

Philosophy 1–2, 5, 11, 15, 18–20, 24, 28, 41, 48, 53, 64, 73, 75–76, 78, 94, 96, 105

Philosophy-of-Life 57

Photons 61

Physical Comforts 96

Physical Constituents 103

Physical Constraints 8

Physical Destruction 2

Physical Environment 2, 35, 38, 42, 62, 104

Physical Existence 1, 21, 38, 74, 97

Physical Health 27

Physicalism 104–105

Physical Laws 60

Physical Material 2, 51, 104

Physical Matter 2, 13

Physical-Mental 62

Physical Nature 43, 77, 104–105

Physical Needs 10, 37, 65–67, 70

Physical Power 12

Physical Sciences 59

Physical Sustenance 33, 66

Physical World 2, 62, 76

Physical "Life-Space 24

Physicist 35, 41, 55, 60

Physicists 23, 48–49, 55, 103

Physics 1–2, 7, 51–52, 56, 59–60, 76

Physiological 24

Physiology 3, 100

Pil 19, 83–85, 89–92, 104

Pluralism 12, 57, 59, 62–64, 96, 104–105

Pof 91

Polkinghorne 41, 52

Post-Solar 7

Post-Traumatic 89

Pragmatic Pluralism 12, 57, 59, 63–64, 96, 105

Pragmatic Reality 48

Pragmatism 62

Preon 54–55

Protoconsciousness 53, 54, 104–105

Prouix 91
Psi Energy 52
Psychiatrist 19, 24, 29, 33, 83
Psychic Experiences 42
Psychic Phenomena 52
Psychism 38
Psychoanalysis 86
Psychokinesis 56
Psychological 26, 33, 42, 44, 68, 88
Psychologies 17
Psychologist 33, 42–43, 53, 89–90, 92–93
Psychologists 91
Psychology of Motivation 66
Psychology of Religion 26
Psychology of Religion and Spirituality 26
Psychology of Religion By Spilka 26
Psychometric Techniques 26
Psychons 55
Psychosocial 44, 87
Psychotherapist 24
Psychotherapy 43
Purpose In Life 19, 83, 85–88, 91, 97, 104
Purpose-In-Life 83, 87

# Q

Quantum Level 60
Quantum Mechanics 56, 59–60
Quantum Mind 56, 60
Quantum Physics 2, 52
Quantum Theory 25, 55–56
Quarks 55, 61
Quarks, Leptons 61

Quasi-Religious 14, 25
Quest 29

# R

Racism 10
Radin 3, 52, 56
Radio 80
Radiologist 24
Rasmussen 84
Real 30, 37, 45
Realism 14
Reker 84
Religion 2, 11–12, 14–15, 21, 25–28, 36, 40, 52, 56, 63–64, 75,
    78–79, 88, 91, 105
Reorientation 57
Robinson 52
Rokeach Value Survey 84
Rollo May 33
Roman Catholic 15
Roy Baumeister 92
Rue 53

# S

Sacredness 14, 25
Sallee and Casciani 85
Science-Religion 16
Scott Kaufman 43
Seager 53
Self-Actualization 85
Self-Actualize 44
Self-Centered 57, 79, 96

Self-Concept 84–85
Self-Concordance 89
Self-Defense 31
Self-Enhancement 20, 28, 71
Self-Fulfillment 66
Self-Ideal 86
Self-Organization 25
Self-Preservation 31
Self-Realization 89
Self-Sacrifice 31
Seligman 11, 17, 88–89
Severin 17
Shah 1
Shamanism 5, 95
Shaver 90–91
Shrader 84
Simpson 75
Socioeconomic 84
Sociology 4, 11, 59, 96, 100
Soderstrom 84
Soderstrom and Wright 84
Sop 86–87, 90–91, 105
Space 23, 51, 61
Space-Time 60
Spilka 26
Spiritual 10, 12, 21, 25–27, 29, 32, 36, 42, 57, 78, 80, 84
Spiritualism 38
Spirituality 10, 14, 21, 23, 26–39, 76, 93–94, 105
Staune 94
Steger, Frazier, Oishi, & Kaler 91
Step 37, 42, 89, 101
Stephen Knapp 30

Stevens, Pfast & Wessels 84
Subatomic Activity 59
Subatomic Constituents 61
Subconscious Mind 18, 35, 69, 78, 87
Suicide 20, 43, 65, 71, 79
Sun 1–2, 41
Superego 43
Superhuman 40
Supermind 60
Super-Mind 7
Supernatural 5–6, 10, 25, 28, 31, 35, 46, 49, 52, 59, 62–63, 74, 78, 94–95, 100, 105
Supernaturalism 28, 56
Superposition 60
Sygons 55
Systems 3, 5–6, 9, 17, 34, 37, 68–69, 78, 86, 95, 100
Szocik 59

# T

Taoism 5
Teilhard De Chardin 41, 75, 80
Teleology 73
Telepathy 56
Term 10–11, 14, 17–18, 20–21, 24, 26–27, 31, 34, 42, 46, 52, 54–56, 63, 67, 83, 89–91, 96, 103–104
Terms 18, 30, 46, 54–56, 103
Theism 52, 63, 105
Theistic 17, 19, 52–53
Theistically 31
Theologian 31, 41
Theologian, John Polkinghorne 41
Theologian Gordon Kaufman 31

Theology 1, 30, 41, 75, 88
Theoretical Physicist 35
Theoretical Physicists 55
Theoretical Physics 51
Theories 15, 19, 36, 42, 44, 51, 53, 59, 66–67, 92
Theory 23–25, 33, 41, 44, 53–56, 63, 66–67, 69, 86, 88–89, 91–92
Theosophy 25
Tirosh-Samuelson 40
Toler 87
Tolerance 12–13, 16, 29, 64, 92
Transcendence 1, 26, 28, 38–40, 42–44, 67, 76, 105
Transcendent Actualization 67, 70
Transcendent Actualizers 35, 43
Transcendent Deity 28, 100
Transcendent Divine Realm 12
Transcendent Force 20
Transcendent Intelligence 48
Transcendent Realm 10, 25, 27
Transcendent Supernatural Realm 35
Transhuman 40

# U

Unconscious Mind 34
United States 10, 14–15, 20, 70, 83–84
United States International University 84
Universal Consciousness 52–53, 75
Universal Reality 44, 47, 49
Universal Unitarian 25
Universal-Unitarian Church 14
Universe 2, 10, 19, 32, 41, 45, 52, 59–61, 74, 100
Universes 45, 61, 100

## V

Viktor Frankl 17, 19, 67, 83
Violence 8, 10, 12, 20, 40, 43, 45, 63, 66, 71, 79, 101
Virtual Reality 48

## W

Walker 56, 60
Weissenbacher 41
Well-Being 9, 11, 15, 17, 19–20, 27, 31, 36, 40, 43, 45, 62, 66,
    69, 80–81, 84, 87–92, 96–97, 103
Wheeler 2, 11, 18–19, 34, 37, 47, 52, 55, 63, 88
William James 17, 63, 67

## Y

Yahweh 93
Yarnell 83

## Z

Zero Point 54
Zika 84
Zika & Chamberlain 84
Zoroaster 5
Zygon 14